NOTARY INFORN

Name:	
Address:	
Phone Number:	**Fax Number:**
Email Address:	

LOG BOOK INFORMATION

Log Book Number:	
Start Date:	**End Date:**

NOTARY RECORD

Printed Name and Address of Signer:	Phone Number:		Thumb Print:
Krystal Kiesel	Email:		
	Signer's Signature:		

Service Performed:	Identification:		I.D. Number:	
O Oath	O I.D. Card	O Credible Witness		
☒ Acknowledgment	☒ Drivers License	O Known Personally	Issued By:	
O Jurat	O Passport		Issued Date:	Expiration Date:
O Other:	O Other:			

Document Type:	Date/Time Notarized:	AM	Document Date:	Fee Charged:
Affidavit	Feb 26, 2021	PM		

Printed Name and Address of Witness:	Phone Number:
N/A	Email:
	Witness' Signature:

Comments:	Record Number:
Renewal of Marriage Vows for Catholic Church	1

NOTARY RECORD

Printed Name and Address of Signer:	Phone Number:		Thumb Print:
	Email:		
	Signer's Signature:		

Service Performed:	Identification:		I.D. Number:	
O Oath	O I.D. Card	O Credible Witness		
O Acknowledgment	O Drivers License	O Known Personally	Issued By:	
O Jurat	O Passport		Issued Date:	Expiration Date:
O Other:	O Other:			

Document Type:	Date/Time Notarized:	AM	Document Date:	Fee Charged:
		PM		

Printed Name and Address of Witness:	Phone Number:
	Email:
	Witness' Signature:

Comments:	Record Number:
	2

NOTARY RECORD

Printed Name and Address of Signer:	Phone Number:	Thumb Print:
	Email:	
	Signer's Signature:	

Service Performed:	Identification:	I.D. Number:	
O Oath	O I.D. Card O Credible Witness		
O Acknowledgment	O Drivers License O Known Personally	Issued By:	
O Jurat	O Passport	Issued Date:	Expiration Date:
O Other:	O Other:		

Document Type:	Date/Time Notarized: AM PM	Document Date:	Fee Charged:

Printed Name and Address of Witness:	Phone Number:
	Email:
	Witness' Signature:

| Comments: | Record Number:

3 |
|---|---|

NOTARY RECORD

Printed Name and Address of Signer:	Phone Number:	Thumb Print:
	Email:	
	Signer's Signature:	

Service Performed:	Identification:	I.D. Number:	
O Oath	O I.D. Card O Credible Witness		
O Acknowledgment	O Drivers License O Known Personally	Issued By:	
O Jurat	O Passport	Issued Date:	Expiration Date:
O Other:	O Other:		

Document Type:	Date/Time Notarized: AM PM	Document Date:	Fee Charged:

Printed Name and Address of Witness:	Phone Number:
	Email:
	Witness' Signature:

| Comments: | Record Number:

4 |
|---|---|

NOTARY RECORD

Printed Name and Address of Signer:	Phone Number:	Thumb Print:
	Email:	
	Signer's Signature:	

Service Performed:	Identification:	I.D. Number:	
O Oath	O I.D. Card O Credible Witness		
O Acknowledgment	O Drivers License O Known Personally	Issued By:	
O Jurat	O Passport	Issued Date:	Expiration Date:
O Other:	O Other:		

Document Type:	Date/Time Notarized: AM PM	Document Date:	Fee Charged:

Printed Name and Address of Witness:	Phone Number:
	Email:
	Witness' Signature:

Comments:	Record Number: **5**

NOTARY RECORD

Printed Name and Address of Signer:	Phone Number:	Thumb Print:
	Email:	
	Signer's Signature:	

Service Performed:	Identification:	I.D. Number:	
O Oath	O I.D. Card O Credible Witness		
O Acknowledgment	O Drivers License O Known Personally	Issued By:	
O Jurat	O Passport	Issued Date:	Expiration Date:
O Other:	O Other:		

Document Type:	Date/Time Notarized: AM PM	Document Date:	Fee Charged:

Printed Name and Address of Witness:	Phone Number:
	Email:
	Witness' Signature:

Comments:	Record Number: **6**

NOTARY RECORD

Printed Name and Address of Signer:	Phone Number:	Thumb Print:
	Email:	
	Signer's Signature:	

Service Performed:	Identification:	I.D. Number:	
O Oath	O I.D. Card O Credible Witness		
O Acknowledgment	O Drivers License O Known Personally	Issued By:	
O Jurat	O Passport	Issued Date:	Expiration Date:
O Other:	O Other:		

Document Type:	Date/Time Notarized: AM PM	Document Date:	Fee Charged:

Printed Name and Address of Witness:	Phone Number:
	Email:
	Witness' Signature:

Comments:	Record Number:
	7

NOTARY RECORD

Printed Name and Address of Signer:	Phone Number:	Thumb Print:
	Email:	
	Signer's Signature:	

Service Performed:	Identification:	I.D. Number:	
O Oath	O I.D. Card O Credible Witness		
O Acknowledgment	O Drivers License O Known Personally	Issued By:	
O Jurat	O Passport	Issued Date:	Expiration Date:
O Other:	O Other:		

Document Type:	Date/Time Notarized: AM PM	Document Date:	Fee Charged:

Printed Name and Address of Witness:	Phone Number:
	Email:
	Witness' Signature:

Comments:	Record Number:
	8

NOTARY RECORD

Printed Name and Address of Signer:	Phone Number:	Thumb Print:
	Email:	
	Signer's Signature:	

Service Performed:	Identification:	I.D. Number:	
O Oath	O I.D. Card O Credible Witness		
O Acknowledgment	O Drivers License O Known Personally	Issued By:	
O Jurat	O Passport	Issued Date:	Expiration Date:
O Other:	O Other:		
Document Type:	Date/Time Notarized: AM PM	Document Date:	Fee Charged:

Printed Name and Address of Witness:	Phone Number:
	Email:
	Witness' Signature:

Comments:	Record Number: **9**

NOTARY RECORD

Printed Name and Address of Signer:	Phone Number:	Thumb Print:
	Email:	
	Signer's Signature:	

Service Performed:	Identification:	I.D. Number:	
O Oath	O I.D. Card O Credible Witness		
O Acknowledgment	O Drivers License O Known Personally	Issued By:	
O Jurat	O Passport	Issued Date:	Expiration Date:
O Other:	O Other:		
Document Type:	Date/Time Notarized: AM PM	Document Date:	Fee Charged:

Printed Name and Address of Witness:	Phone Number:
	Email:
	Witness' Signature:

Comments:	Record Number: **10**

NOTARY RECORD

Printed Name and Address of Signer:	Phone Number:	Thumb Print:
	Email:	
	Signer's Signature:	

Service Performed:	Identification:	I.D. Number:	
O Oath	O I.D. Card O Credible Witness		
O Acknowledgment	O Drivers License O Known Personally	Issued By:	
O Jurat	O Passport	Issued Date:	Expiration Date:
O Other:	O Other:		

Document Type:	Date/Time Notarized: AM PM	Document Date:	Fee Charged:

Printed Name and Address of Witness:	Phone Number:
	Email:
	Witness' Signature:

Comments:	Record Number: **11**

NOTARY RECORD

Printed Name and Address of Signer:	Phone Number:	Thumb Print:
	Email:	
	Signer's Signature:	

Service Performed:	Identification:	I.D. Number:	
O Oath	O I.D. Card O Credible Witness		
O Acknowledgment	O Drivers License O Known Personally	Issued By:	
O Jurat	O Passport	Issued Date:	Expiration Date:
O Other:	O Other:		

Document Type:	Date/Time Notarized: AM PM	Document Date:	Fee Charged:

Printed Name and Address of Witness:	Phone Number:
	Email:
	Witness' Signature:

Comments:	Record Number: **12**

NOTARY RECORD

Printed Name and Address of Signer:	Phone Number:	Thumb Print:
	Email:	
	Signer's Signature:	

Service Performed:	Identification:	I.D. Number:	
O Oath	O I.D. Card O Credible Witness		
O Acknowledgment	O Drivers License O Known Personally	Issued By:	
O Jurat	O Passport	Issued Date:	Expiration Date:
O Other:	O Other:		

Document Type:	Date/Time Notarized: AM PM	Document Date:	Fee Charged:

Printed Name and Address of Witness:	Phone Number:
	Email:
	Witness' Signature:

Comments:	Record Number: **13**

NOTARY RECORD

Printed Name and Address of Signer:	Phone Number:	Thumb Print:
	Email:	
	Signer's Signature:	

Service Performed:	Identification:	I.D. Number:	
O Oath	O I.D. Card O Credible Witness		
O Acknowledgment	O Drivers License O Known Personally	Issued By:	
O Jurat	O Passport	Issued Date:	Expiration Date:
O Other:	O Other:		

Document Type:	Date/Time Notarized: AM PM	Document Date:	Fee Charged:

Printed Name and Address of Witness:	Phone Number:
	Email:
	Witness' Signature:

Comments:	Record Number: **14**

NOTARY RECORD

Printed Name and Address of Signer:	Phone Number:		Thumb Print:
	Email:		
	Signer's Signature:		

Service Performed:	Identification:		I.D. Number:	
O Oath	O I.D. Card	O Credible Witness		
O Acknowledgment	O Drivers License	O Known Personally	Issued By:	
O Jurat	O Passport		Issued Date:	Expiration Date:
O Other:	O Other:			

Document Type:	Date/Time Notarized:	AM PM	Document Date:	Fee Charged:

Printed Name and Address of Witness:	Phone Number:
	Email:
	Witness' Signature:

Comments:	Record Number: 15

NOTARY RECORD

Printed Name and Address of Signer:	Phone Number:		Thumb Print:
	Email:		
	Signer's Signature:		

Service Performed:	Identification:		I.D. Number:	
O Oath	O I.D. Card	O Credible Witness		
O Acknowledgment	O Drivers License	O Known Personally	Issued By:	
O Jurat	O Passport		Issued Date:	Expiration Date:
O Other:	O Other:			

Document Type:	Date/Time Notarized:	AM PM	Document Date:	Fee Charged:

Printed Name and Address of Witness:	Phone Number:
	Email:
	Witness' Signature:

Comments:	Record Number: 16

NOTARY RECORD

Printed Name and Address of Signer:	Phone Number:	Thumb Print:
	Email:	
	Signer's Signature:	

Service Performed:	Identification:	I.D. Number:	
O Oath	O I.D. Card O Credible Witness		
O Acknowledgment	O Drivers License O Known Personally	Issued By:	
O Jurat	O Passport	Issued Date:	Expiration Date:
O Other:	O Other:		

Document Type:	Date/Time Notarized: AM PM	Document Date:	Fee Charged:

Printed Name and Address of Witness:	Phone Number:
	Email:
	Witness' Signature:

Comments:	Record Number: **17**

NOTARY RECORD

Printed Name and Address of Signer:	Phone Number:	Thumb Print:
	Email:	
	Signer's Signature:	

Service Performed:	Identification:	I.D. Number:	
O Oath	O I.D. Card O Credible Witness		
O Acknowledgment	O Drivers License O Known Personally	Issued By:	
O Jurat	O Passport	Issued Date:	Expiration Date:
O Other:	O Other:		

Document Type:	Date/Time Notarized: AM PM	Document Date:	Fee Charged:

Printed Name and Address of Witness:	Phone Number:
	Email:
	Witness' Signature:

Comments:	Record Number: **18**

NOTARY RECORD

Printed Name and Address of Signer:	Phone Number:	Thumb Print:
	Email:	
	Signer's Signature:	

Service Performed:	Identification:	I.D. Number:	
O Oath	O I.D. Card O Credible Witness		
O Acknowledgment	O Drivers License O Known Personally	Issued By:	
O Jurat	O Passport	Issued Date:	Expiration Date:
O Other:	O Other:		

Document Type:	Date/Time Notarized: AM PM	Document Date:	Fee Charged:

Printed Name and Address of Witness:	Phone Number:
	Email:
	Witness' Signature:

Comments:	Record Number: 19

NOTARY RECORD

Printed Name and Address of Signer:	Phone Number:	Thumb Print:
	Email:	
	Signer's Signature:	

Service Performed:	Identification:	I.D. Number:	
O Oath	O I.D. Card O Credible Witness		
O Acknowledgment	O Drivers License O Known Personally	Issued By:	
O Jurat	O Passport	Issued Date:	Expiration Date:
O Other:	O Other:		

Document Type:	Date/Time Notarized: AM PM	Document Date:	Fee Charged:

Printed Name and Address of Witness:	Phone Number:
	Email:
	Witness' Signature:

Comments:	Record Number: 20

NOTARY RECORD

Printed Name and Address of Signer:	Phone Number:	Thumb Print:
	Email:	
	Signer's Signature:	

Service Performed:	Identification:	I.D. Number:	
O Oath	O I.D. Card O Credible Witness		
O Acknowledgment	O Drivers License O Known Personally	Issued By:	
O Jurat	O Passport	Issued Date:	Expiration Date:
O Other:	O Other:		

Document Type:	Date/Time Notarized: AM PM	Document Date:	Fee Charged:

Printed Name and Address of Witness:	Phone Number:
	Email:
	Witness' Signature:

Comments:	Record Number: **21**

NOTARY RECORD

Printed Name and Address of Signer:	Phone Number:	Thumb Print:
	Email:	
	Signer's Signature:	

Service Performed:	Identification:	I.D. Number:	
O Oath	O I.D. Card O Credible Witness		
O Acknowledgment	O Drivers License O Known Personally	Issued By:	
O Jurat	O Passport	Issued Date:	Expiration Date:
O Other:	O Other:		

Document Type:	Date/Time Notarized: AM PM	Document Date:	Fee Charged:

Printed Name and Address of Witness:	Phone Number:
	Email:
	Witness' Signature:

Comments:	Record Number: **22**

NOTARY RECORD

Printed Name and Address of Signer:	Phone Number:	Thumb Print:
	Email:	
	Signer's Signature:	

Service Performed:	Identification:	I.D. Number:	
O Oath	O I.D. Card　　O Credible Witness		
O Acknowledgment	O Drivers License　O Known Personally	Issued By:	
O Jurat	O Passport		
O Other:	O Other:	Issued Date:	Expiration Date:

Document Type:	Date/Time Notarized:　　AM　PM	Document Date:	Fee Charged:

Printed Name and Address of Witness:	Phone Number:
	Email:
	Witness' Signature:

Comments:	Record Number: **23**

NOTARY RECORD

Printed Name and Address of Signer:	Phone Number:	Thumb Print:
	Email:	
	Signer's Signature:	

Service Performed:	Identification:	I.D. Number:	
O Oath	O I.D. Card　　O Credible Witness		
O Acknowledgment	O Drivers License　O Known Personally	Issued By:	
O Jurat	O Passport		
O Other:	O Other:	Issued Date:	Expiration Date:

Document Type:	Date/Time Notarized:　　AM　PM	Document Date:	Fee Charged:

Printed Name and Address of Witness:	Phone Number:
	Email:
	Witness' Signature:

Comments:	Record Number: **24**

NOTARY RECORD

Printed Name and Address of Signer:	Phone Number:	Thumb Print:
	Email:	
	Signer's Signature:	

Service Performed:	Identification:	I.D. Number:	
O Oath	O I.D. Card O Credible Witness		
O Acknowledgment	O Drivers License O Known Personally	Issued By:	
O Jurat	O Passport	Issued Date:	Expiration Date:
O Other:	O Other:		

Document Type:	Date/Time Notarized: AM PM	Document Date:	Fee Charged:

Printed Name and Address of Witness:	Phone Number:
	Email:
	Witness' Signature:

Comments:	Record Number: **25**

NOTARY RECORD

Printed Name and Address of Signer:	Phone Number:	Thumb Print:
	Email:	
	Signer's Signature:	

Service Performed:	Identification:	I.D. Number:	
O Oath	O I.D. Card O Credible Witness		
O Acknowledgment	O Drivers License O Known Personally	Issued By:	
O Jurat	O Passport	Issued Date:	Expiration Date:
O Other:	O Other:		

Document Type:	Date/Time Notarized: AM PM	Document Date:	Fee Charged:

Printed Name and Address of Witness:	Phone Number:
	Email:
	Witness' Signature:

Comments:	Record Number: **26**

NOTARY RECORD

Printed Name and Address of Signer:	Phone Number:	Thumb Print:
	Email:	
	Signer's Signature:	

Service Performed:	Identification:	I.D. Number:	
O Oath	O I.D. Card O Credible Witness		
O Acknowledgment	O Drivers License O Known Personally	Issued By:	
O Jurat	O Passport	Issued Date:	Expiration Date:
O Other:	O Other:		
Document Type:	Date/Time Notarized: AM PM	Document Date:	Fee Charged:

Printed Name and Address of Witness:	Phone Number:
	Email:
	Witness' Signature:

Comments:	Record Number: 27

NOTARY RECORD

Printed Name and Address of Signer:	Phone Number:	Thumb Print:
	Email:	
	Signer's Signature:	

Service Performed:	Identification:	I.D. Number:	
O Oath	O I.D. Card O Credible Witness		
O Acknowledgment	O Drivers License O Known Personally	Issued By:	
O Jurat	O Passport	Issued Date:	Expiration Date:
O Other:	O Other:		
Document Type:	Date/Time Notarized: AM PM	Document Date:	Fee Charged:

Printed Name and Address of Witness:	Phone Number:
	Email:
	Witness' Signature:

Comments:	Record Number: 28

NOTARY RECORD

Printed Name and Address of Signer:	Phone Number:	Thumb Print:
	Email:	
	Signer's Signature:	

Service Performed:	Identification:	I.D. Number:	
O Oath	O I.D. Card O Credible Witness		
O Acknowledgment	O Drivers License O Known Personally	Issued By:	
O Jurat	O Passport		
O Other:	O Other:	Issued Date:	Expiration Date:

Document Type:	Date/Time Notarized: AM PM	Document Date:	Fee Charged:

Printed Name and Address of Witness:	Phone Number:
	Email:
	Witness' Signature:

Comments:	Record Number: **29**

NOTARY RECORD

Printed Name and Address of Signer:	Phone Number:	Thumb Print:
	Email:	
	Signer's Signature:	

Service Performed:	Identification:	I.D. Number:	
O Oath	O I.D. Card O Credible Witness		
O Acknowledgment	O Drivers License O Known Personally	Issued By:	
O Jurat	O Passport		
O Other:	O Other:	Issued Date:	Expiration Date:

Document Type:	Date/Time Notarized: AM PM	Document Date:	Fee Charged:

Printed Name and Address of Witness:	Phone Number:
	Email:
	Witness' Signature:

Comments:	Record Number: **30**

NOTARY RECORD

Printed Name and Address of Signer:	Phone Number:	Thumb Print:
	Email:	
	Signer's Signature:	

Service Performed:	Identification:	I.D. Number:	
O Oath	O I.D. Card O Credible Witness		
O Acknowledgment	O Drivers License O Known Personally	Issued By:	
O Jurat	O Passport	Issued Date:	Expiration Date:
O Other:	O Other:		

Document Type:	Date/Time Notarized: AM PM	Document Date:	Fee Charged:

Printed Name and Address of Witness:	Phone Number:
	Email:
	Witness' Signature:

Comments:	Record Number: **31**

NOTARY RECORD

Printed Name and Address of Signer:	Phone Number:	Thumb Print:
	Email:	
	Signer's Signature:	

Service Performed:	Identification:	I.D. Number:	
O Oath	O I.D. Card O Credible Witness		
O Acknowledgment	O Drivers License O Known Personally	Issued By:	
O Jurat	O Passport	Issued Date:	Expiration Date:
O Other:	O Other:		

Document Type:	Date/Time Notarized: AM PM	Document Date:	Fee Charged:

Printed Name and Address of Witness:	Phone Number:
	Email:
	Witness' Signature:

Comments:	Record Number: **32**

NOTARY RECORD

Printed Name and Address of Signer:	Phone Number:	Thumb Print:
	Email:	
	Signer's Signature:	

Service Performed:	Identification:	I.D. Number:	
O Oath	O I.D. Card O Credible Witness		
O Acknowledgment	O Drivers License O Known Personally	Issued By:	
O Jurat	O Passport	Issued Date:	Expiration Date:
O Other:	O Other:		

Document Type:	Date/Time Notarized: AM PM	Document Date:	Fee Charged:

Printed Name and Address of Witness:	Phone Number:
	Email:
	Witness' Signature:

Comments:	Record Number: **33**

NOTARY RECORD

Printed Name and Address of Signer:	Phone Number:	Thumb Print:
	Email:	
	Signer's Signature:	

Service Performed:	Identification:	I.D. Number:	
O Oath	O I.D. Card O Credible Witness		
O Acknowledgment	O Drivers License O Known Personally	Issued By:	
O Jurat	O Passport	Issued Date:	Expiration Date:
O Other:	O Other:		

Document Type:	Date/Time Notarized: AM PM	Document Date:	Fee Charged:

Printed Name and Address of Witness:	Phone Number:
	Email:
	Witness' Signature:

Comments:	Record Number: **34**

NOTARY RECORD

Printed Name and Address of Signer:	Phone Number:		Thumb Print:
	Email:		
	Signer's Signature:		

Service Performed:	Identification:		I.D. Number:	
O Oath	O I.D. Card	O Credible Witness		
O Acknowledgment	O Drivers License	O Known Personally	Issued By:	
O Jurat	O Passport		Issued Date:	Expiration Date:
O Other:	O Other:			

Document Type:	Date/Time Notarized: AM PM	Document Date:	Fee Charged:

Printed Name and Address of Witness:	Phone Number:
	Email:
	Witness' Signature:

Comments:	Record Number: **35**

NOTARY RECORD

Printed Name and Address of Signer:	Phone Number:		Thumb Print:
	Email:		
	Signer's Signature:		

Service Performed:	Identification:		I.D. Number:	
O Oath	O I.D. Card	O Credible Witness		
O Acknowledgment	O Drivers License	O Known Personally	Issued By:	
O Jurat	O Passport		Issued Date:	Expiration Date:
O Other:	O Other:			

Document Type:	Date/Time Notarized: AM PM	Document Date:	Fee Charged:

Printed Name and Address of Witness:	Phone Number:
	Email:
	Witness' Signature:

Comments:	Record Number: **36**

NOTARY RECORD

Printed Name and Address of Signer:	Phone Number:	Thumb Print:
	Email:	
	Signer's Signature:	

Service Performed:	Identification:	I.D. Number:
O Oath	O I.D. Card O Credible Witness	
O Acknowledgment	O Drivers License O Known Personally	Issued By:
O Jurat	O Passport	Issued Date: Expiration Date:
O Other:	O Other:	

Document Type:	Date/Time Notarized: AM PM	Document Date:	Fee Charged:

Printed Name and Address of Witness:	Phone Number:
	Email:
	Witness' Signature:

Comments:	Record Number: **37**

NOTARY RECORD

Printed Name and Address of Signer:	Phone Number:	Thumb Print:
	Email:	
	Signer's Signature:	

Service Performed:	Identification:	I.D. Number:
O Oath	O I.D. Card O Credible Witness	
O Acknowledgment	O Drivers License O Known Personally	Issued By:
O Jurat	O Passport	Issued Date: Expiration Date:
O Other:	O Other:	

Document Type:	Date/Time Notarized: AM PM	Document Date:	Fee Charged:

Printed Name and Address of Witness:	Phone Number:
	Email:
	Witness' Signature:

Comments:	Record Number: **38**

NOTARY RECORD

Printed Name and Address of Signer:	Phone Number:	Thumb Print:
	Email:	
	Signer's Signature:	

Service Performed:
- O Oath
- O Acknowledgment
- O Jurat
- O Other:

Identification:
- O I.D. Card
- O Drivers License
- O Passport
- O Other:
- O Credible Witness
- O Known Personally

I.D. Number:	
Issued By:	
Issued Date:	Expiration Date:

Document Type:	Date/Time Notarized: AM PM	Document Date:	Fee Charged:

Printed Name and Address of Witness:	Phone Number:
	Email:
	Witness' Signature:

Comments:	Record Number: **39**

NOTARY RECORD

Printed Name and Address of Signer:	Phone Number:	Thumb Print:
	Email:	
	Signer's Signature:	

Service Performed:
- O Oath
- O Acknowledgment
- O Jurat
- O Other:

Identification:
- O I.D. Card
- O Drivers License
- O Passport
- O Other:
- O Credible Witness
- O Known Personally

I.D. Number:	
Issued By:	
Issued Date:	Expiration Date:

Document Type:	Date/Time Notarized: AM PM	Document Date:	Fee Charged:

Printed Name and Address of Witness:	Phone Number:
	Email:
	Witness' Signature:

Comments:	Record Number: **40**

NOTARY RECORD

Printed Name and Address of Signer:	Phone Number:	Thumb Print:
	Email:	
	Signer's Signature:	

Service Performed:	Identification:	I.D. Number:	
O Oath	O I.D. Card O Credible Witness		
O Acknowledgment	O Drivers License O Known Personally	Issued By:	
O Jurat	O Passport	Issued Date:	Expiration Date:
O Other:	O Other:		

Document Type:	Date/Time Notarized: AM PM	Document Date:	Fee Charged:

Printed Name and Address of Witness:	Phone Number:
	Email:
	Witness' Signature:

Comments:	Record Number: 41

NOTARY RECORD

Printed Name and Address of Signer:	Phone Number:	Thumb Print:
	Email:	
	Signer's Signature:	

Service Performed:	Identification:	I.D. Number:	
O Oath	O I.D. Card O Credible Witness		
O Acknowledgment	O Drivers License O Known Personally	Issued By:	
O Jurat	O Passport	Issued Date:	Expiration Date:
O Other:	O Other:		

Document Type:	Date/Time Notarized: AM PM	Document Date:	Fee Charged:

Printed Name and Address of Witness:	Phone Number:
	Email:
	Witness' Signature:

Comments:	Record Number: 42

NOTARY RECORD

Printed Name and Address of Signer:	Phone Number:	Thumb Print:
	Email:	
	Signer's Signature:	

Service Performed:	Identification:	I.D. Number:	
O Oath	O I.D. Card O Credible Witness		
O Acknowledgment	O Drivers License O Known Personally	Issued By:	
O Jurat	O Passport	Issued Date:	Expiration Date:
O Other:	O Other:		
Document Type:	Date/Time Notarized: AM PM	Document Date:	Fee Charged:

Printed Name and Address of Witness:	Phone Number:
	Email:
	Witness' Signature:

Comments:	Record Number: **43**

NOTARY RECORD

Printed Name and Address of Signer:	Phone Number:	Thumb Print:
	Email:	
	Signer's Signature:	

Service Performed:	Identification:	I.D. Number:	
O Oath	O I.D. Card O Credible Witness		
O Acknowledgment	O Drivers License O Known Personally	Issued By:	
O Jurat	O Passport	Issued Date:	Expiration Date:
O Other:	O Other:		
Document Type:	Date/Time Notarized: AM PM	Document Date:	Fee Charged:

Printed Name and Address of Witness:	Phone Number:
	Email:
	Witness' Signature:

Comments:	Record Number: **44**

NOTARY RECORD

Printed Name and Address of Signer:	Phone Number:	Thumb Print:
	Email:	
	Signer's Signature:	

Service Performed:	Identification:	I.D. Number:	
O Oath	O I.D. Card O Credible Witness		
O Acknowledgment	O Drivers License O Known Personally	Issued By:	
O Jurat	O Passport	Issued Date:	Expiration Date:
O Other:	O Other:		

Document Type:	Date/Time Notarized:	AM PM	Document Date:	Fee Charged:

Printed Name and Address of Witness:	Phone Number:
	Email:
	Witness' Signature:

Comments:	Record Number:
	45

NOTARY RECORD

Printed Name and Address of Signer:	Phone Number:	Thumb Print:
	Email:	
	Signer's Signature:	

Service Performed:	Identification:	I.D. Number:	
O Oath	O I.D. Card O Credible Witness		
O Acknowledgment	O Drivers License O Known Personally	Issued By:	
O Jurat	O Passport	Issued Date:	Expiration Date:
O Other:	O Other:		

Document Type:	Date/Time Notarized:	AM PM	Document Date:	Fee Charged:

Printed Name and Address of Witness:	Phone Number:
	Email:
	Witness' Signature:

Comments:	Record Number:
	46

NOTARY RECORD

Printed Name and Address of Signer:

Phone Number:

Email:

Signer's Signature:

Thumb Print:

Service Performed:
- O Oath
- O Acknowledgment
- O Jurat
- O Other:

Identification:
- O I.D. Card
- O Drivers License
- O Passport
- O Other:

- O Credible Witness
- O Known Personally

I.D. Number:

Issued By:

Issued Date:

Expiration Date:

Document Type:

Date/Time Notarized: AM PM

Document Date:

Fee Charged:

Printed Name and Address of Witness:

Phone Number:

Email:

Witness' Signature:

Comments:

Record Number:
47

NOTARY RECORD

Printed Name and Address of Signer:

Phone Number:

Email:

Signer's Signature:

Thumb Print:

Service Performed:
- O Oath
- O Acknowledgment
- O Jurat
- O Other:

Identification:
- O I.D. Card
- O Drivers License
- O Passport
- O Other:

- O Credible Witness
- O Known Personally

I.D. Number:

Issued By:

Issued Date:

Expiration Date:

Document Type:

Date/Time Notarized: AM PM

Document Date:

Fee Charged:

Printed Name and Address of Witness:

Phone Number:

Email:

Witness' Signature:

Comments:

Record Number:
48

NOTARY RECORD

Printed Name and Address of Signer:	Phone Number:	Thumb Print:
	Email:	
	Signer's Signature:	

Service Performed:	Identification:	I.D. Number:	
O Oath	O I.D. Card O Credible Witness		
O Acknowledgment	O Drivers License O Known Personally	Issued By:	
O Jurat	O Passport	Issued Date:	Expiration Date:
O Other:	O Other:		

Document Type:	Date/Time Notarized: AM PM	Document Date:	Fee Charged:

Printed Name and Address of Witness:	Phone Number:
	Email:
	Witness' Signature:

Comments:	Record Number: **49**

NOTARY RECORD

Printed Name and Address of Signer:	Phone Number:	Thumb Print:
	Email:	
	Signer's Signature:	

Service Performed:	Identification:	I.D. Number:	
O Oath	O I.D. Card O Credible Witness		
O Acknowledgment	O Drivers License O Known Personally	Issued By:	
O Jurat	O Passport	Issued Date:	Expiration Date:
O Other:	O Other:		

Document Type:	Date/Time Notarized: AM PM	Document Date:	Fee Charged:

Printed Name and Address of Witness:	Phone Number:
	Email:
	Witness' Signature:

Comments:	Record Number: **50**

NOTARY RECORD

Printed Name and Address of Signer:	Phone Number:	Thumb Print:
	Email:	
	Signer's Signature:	

Service Performed:	Identification:	I.D. Number:	
O Oath	O I.D. Card O Credible Witness		
O Acknowledgment	O Drivers License O Known Personally	Issued By:	
O Jurat	O Passport	Issued Date:	Expiration Date:
O Other:	O Other:		

Document Type:	Date/Time Notarized: AM PM	Document Date:	Fee Charged:

Printed Name and Address of Witness:	Phone Number:
	Email:
	Witness' Signature:

Comments:	Record Number: 51

NOTARY RECORD

Printed Name and Address of Signer:	Phone Number:	Thumb Print:
	Email:	
	Signer's Signature:	

Service Performed:	Identification:	I.D. Number:	
O Oath	O I.D. Card O Credible Witness		
O Acknowledgment	O Drivers License O Known Personally	Issued By:	
O Jurat	O Passport	Issued Date:	Expiration Date:
O Other:	O Other:		

Document Type:	Date/Time Notarized: AM PM	Document Date:	Fee Charged:

Printed Name and Address of Witness:	Phone Number:
	Email:
	Witness' Signature:

Comments:	Record Number: 52

NOTARY RECORD

Printed Name and Address of Signer:	Phone Number:	Thumb Print:
	Email:	
	Signer's Signature:	

Service Performed:	Identification:	I.D. Number:	
O Oath	O I.D. Card O Credible Witness		
O Acknowledgment	O Drivers License O Known Personally	Issued By:	
O Jurat	O Passport		
O Other:	O Other:	Issued Date:	Expiration Date:

Document Type:	Date/Time Notarized: AM PM	Document Date:	Fee Charged:

Printed Name and Address of Witness:	Phone Number:
	Email:
	Witness' Signature:

Comments:	Record Number:
	53

NOTARY RECORD

Printed Name and Address of Signer:	Phone Number:	Thumb Print:
	Email:	
	Signer's Signature:	

Service Performed:	Identification:	I.D. Number:	
O Oath	O I.D. Card O Credible Witness		
O Acknowledgment	O Drivers License O Known Personally	Issued By:	
O Jurat	O Passport		
O Other:	O Other:	Issued Date:	Expiration Date:

Document Type:	Date/Time Notarized: AM PM	Document Date:	Fee Charged:

Printed Name and Address of Witness:	Phone Number:
	Email:
	Witness' Signature:

Comments:	Record Number:
	54

NOTARY RECORD

Printed Name and Address of Signer:	Phone Number:	Thumb Print:
	Email:	
	Signer's Signature:	

Service Performed:	Identification:	I.D. Number:	
O Oath	O I.D. Card O Credible Witness		
O Acknowledgment	O Drivers License O Known Personally	Issued By:	
O Jurat	O Passport	Issued Date:	Expiration Date:
O Other:	O Other:		

Document Type:	Date/Time Notarized: AM PM	Document Date:	Fee Charged:

Printed Name and Address of Witness:	Phone Number:
	Email:
	Witness' Signature:

Comments:	Record Number:
	55

NOTARY RECORD

Printed Name and Address of Signer:	Phone Number:	Thumb Print:
	Email:	
	Signer's Signature:	

Service Performed:	Identification:	I.D. Number:	
O Oath	O I.D. Card O Credible Witness		
O Acknowledgment	O Drivers License O Known Personally	Issued By:	
O Jurat	O Passport	Issued Date:	Expiration Date:
O Other:	O Other:		

Document Type:	Date/Time Notarized: AM PM	Document Date:	Fee Charged:

Printed Name and Address of Witness:	Phone Number:
	Email:
	Witness' Signature:

Comments:	Record Number:
	56

NOTARY RECORD

Printed Name and Address of Signer:	Phone Number:	Thumb Print:
	Email:	
	Signer's Signature:	

Service Performed:	Identification:	I.D. Number:	
O Oath	O I.D. Card O Credible Witness		
O Acknowledgment	O Drivers License O Known Personally	Issued By:	
O Jurat	O Passport		
O Other:	O Other:	Issued Date:	Expiration Date:

Document Type:	Date/Time Notarized: AM PM	Document Date:	Fee Charged:

Printed Name and Address of Witness:	Phone Number:
	Email:
	Witness' Signature:

Comments:	Record Number: **57**

NOTARY RECORD

Printed Name and Address of Signer:	Phone Number:	Thumb Print:
	Email:	
	Signer's Signature:	

Service Performed:	Identification:	I.D. Number:	
O Oath	O I.D. Card O Credible Witness		
O Acknowledgment	O Drivers License O Known Personally	Issued By:	
O Jurat	O Passport		
O Other:	O Other:	Issued Date:	Expiration Date:

Document Type:	Date/Time Notarized: AM PM	Document Date:	Fee Charged:

Printed Name and Address of Witness:	Phone Number:
	Email:
	Witness' Signature:

Comments:	Record Number: **58**

NOTARY RECORD

Printed Name and Address of Signer:	Phone Number:	Thumb Print:
	Email:	
	Signer's Signature:	

Service Performed:	Identification:	I.D. Number:	
O Oath	O I.D. Card O Credible Witness		
O Acknowledgment	O Drivers License O Known Personally	Issued By:	
O Jurat	O Passport	Issued Date:	Expiration Date:
O Other:	O Other:		

Document Type:	Date/Time Notarized: AM PM	Document Date:	Fee Charged:

Printed Name and Address of Witness:	Phone Number:
	Email:
	Witness' Signature:

Comments:	Record Number: **59**

NOTARY RECORD

Printed Name and Address of Signer:	Phone Number:	Thumb Print:
	Email:	
	Signer's Signature:	

Service Performed:	Identification:	I.D. Number:	
O Oath	O I.D. Card O Credible Witness		
O Acknowledgment	O Drivers License O Known Personally	Issued By:	
O Jurat	O Passport	Issued Date:	Expiration Date:
O Other:	O Other:		

Document Type:	Date/Time Notarized: AM PM	Document Date:	Fee Charged:

Printed Name and Address of Witness:	Phone Number:
	Email:
	Witness' Signature:

Comments:	Record Number: **60**

NOTARY RECORD

Printed Name and Address of Signer:	Phone Number:		Thumb Print:
	Email:		
	Signer's Signature:		

Service Performed:	Identification:		I.D. Number:	
O Oath	O I.D. Card	O Credible Witness		
O Acknowledgment	O Drivers License	O Known Personally	Issued By:	
O Jurat	O Passport		Issued Date:	Expiration Date:
O Other:	O Other:			

Document Type:	Date/Time Notarized:	AM PM	Document Date:	Fee Charged:

Printed Name and Address of Witness:	Phone Number:
	Email:
	Witness' Signature:

Comments:	Record Number: 61

NOTARY RECORD

Printed Name and Address of Signer:	Phone Number:		Thumb Print:
	Email:		
	Signer's Signature:		

Service Performed:	Identification:		I.D. Number:	
O Oath	O I.D. Card	O Credible Witness		
O Acknowledgment	O Drivers License	O Known Personally	Issued By:	
O Jurat	O Passport		Issued Date:	Expiration Date:
O Other:	O Other:			

Document Type:	Date/Time Notarized:	AM PM	Document Date:	Fee Charged:

Printed Name and Address of Witness:	Phone Number:
	Email:
	Witness' Signature:

Comments:	Record Number: 62

NOTARY RECORD

Printed Name and Address of Signer:	Phone Number:	Thumb Print:
	Email:	
	Signer's Signature:	

Service Performed:	Identification:	I.D. Number:	
O Oath	O I.D. Card O Credible Witness		
O Acknowledgment	O Drivers License O Known Personally	Issued By:	
O Jurat	O Passport	Issued Date:	Expiration Date:
O Other:	O Other:		

Document Type:	Date/Time Notarized: AM PM	Document Date:	Fee Charged:

Printed Name and Address of Witness:	Phone Number:
	Email:
	Witness' Signature:

Comments:	Record Number: **63**

NOTARY RECORD

Printed Name and Address of Signer:	Phone Number:	Thumb Print:
	Email:	
	Signer's Signature:	

Service Performed:	Identification:	I.D. Number:	
O Oath	O I.D. Card O Credible Witness		
O Acknowledgment	O Drivers License O Known Personally	Issued By:	
O Jurat	O Passport	Issued Date:	Expiration Date:
O Other:	O Other:		

Document Type:	Date/Time Notarized: AM PM	Document Date:	Fee Charged:

Printed Name and Address of Witness:	Phone Number:
	Email:
	Witness' Signature:

Comments:	Record Number: **64**

NOTARY RECORD

Printed Name and Address of Signer:	Phone Number:	Thumb Print:
	Email:	
	Signer's Signature:	

Service Performed:	Identification:	I.D. Number:	
O Oath	O I.D. Card O Credible Witness		
O Acknowledgment	O Drivers License O Known Personally	Issued By:	
O Jurat	O Passport	Issued Date:	Expiration Date:
O Other:	O Other:		

Document Type:	Date/Time Notarized: AM PM	Document Date:	Fee Charged:

Printed Name and Address of Witness:	Phone Number:
	Email:
	Witness' Signature:

Comments:	Record Number: **65**

NOTARY RECORD

Printed Name and Address of Signer:	Phone Number:	Thumb Print:
	Email:	
	Signer's Signature:	

Service Performed:	Identification:	I.D. Number:	
O Oath	O I.D. Card O Credible Witness		
O Acknowledgment	O Drivers License O Known Personally	Issued By:	
O Jurat	O Passport	Issued Date:	Expiration Date:
O Other:	O Other:		

Document Type:	Date/Time Notarized: AM PM	Document Date:	Fee Charged:

Printed Name and Address of Witness:	Phone Number:
	Email:
	Witness' Signature:

Comments:	Record Number: **66**

NOTARY RECORD

Printed Name and Address of Signer:	Phone Number:	Thumb Print:
	Email:	
	Signer's Signature:	

Service Performed:	Identification:	I.D. Number:	
O Oath	O I.D. Card O Credible Witness		
O Acknowledgment	O Drivers License O Known Personally	Issued By:	
O Jurat	O Passport	Issued Date:	Expiration Date:
O Other:	O Other:		

Document Type:	Date/Time Notarized: AM PM	Document Date:	Fee Charged:

Printed Name and Address of Witness:	Phone Number:
	Email:
	Witness' Signature:

Comments:	Record Number: **67**

NOTARY RECORD

Printed Name and Address of Signer:	Phone Number:	Thumb Print:
	Email:	
	Signer's Signature:	

Service Performed:	Identification:	I.D. Number:	
O Oath	O I.D. Card O Credible Witness		
O Acknowledgment	O Drivers License O Known Personally	Issued By:	
O Jurat	O Passport	Issued Date:	Expiration Date:
O Other:	O Other:		

Document Type:	Date/Time Notarized: AM PM	Document Date:	Fee Charged:

Printed Name and Address of Witness:	Phone Number:
	Email:
	Witness' Signature:

Comments:	Record Number: **68**

NOTARY RECORD

Printed Name and Address of Signer:	Phone Number:	Thumb Print:
	Email:	
	Signer's Signature:	

Service Performed:
- O Oath
- O Acknowledgment
- O Jurat
- O Other:

Identification:
- O I.D. Card   O Credible Witness
- O Drivers License   O Known Personally
- O Passport
- O Other:

I.D. Number:

Issued By:

Issued Date: **Expiration Date:**

Document Type:	Date/Time Notarized: AM PM	Document Date:	Fee Charged:

Printed Name and Address of Witness:	Phone Number:
	Email:
	Witness' Signature:

Comments:	Record Number: **69**

NOTARY RECORD

Printed Name and Address of Signer:	Phone Number:	Thumb Print:
	Email:	
	Signer's Signature:	

Service Performed:
- O Oath
- O Acknowledgment
- O Jurat
- O Other:

Identification:
- O I.D. Card   O Credible Witness
- O Drivers License   O Known Personally
- O Passport
- O Other:

I.D. Number:

Issued By:

Issued Date: **Expiration Date:**

Document Type:	Date/Time Notarized: AM PM	Document Date:	Fee Charged:

Printed Name and Address of Witness:	Phone Number:
	Email:
	Witness' Signature:

Comments:	Record Number: **70**

NOTARY RECORD

Printed Name and Address of Signer:	Phone Number:	Thumb Print:
	Email:	
	Signer's Signature:	

Service Performed:	Identification:	I.D. Number:	
O Oath	O I.D. Card O Credible Witness		
O Acknowledgment	O Drivers License O Known Personally	Issued By:	
O Jurat	O Passport		
O Other:	O Other:	Issued Date:	Expiration Date:

Document Type:	Date/Time Notarized: AM PM	Document Date:	Fee Charged:

Printed Name and Address of Witness:	Phone Number:
	Email:
	Witness' Signature:

Comments:	Record Number: 71

NOTARY RECORD

Printed Name and Address of Signer:	Phone Number:	Thumb Print:
	Email:	
	Signer's Signature:	

Service Performed:	Identification:	I.D. Number:	
O Oath	O I.D. Card O Credible Witness		
O Acknowledgment	O Drivers License O Known Personally	Issued By:	
O Jurat	O Passport		
O Other:	O Other:	Issued Date:	Expiration Date:

Document Type:	Date/Time Notarized: AM PM	Document Date:	Fee Charged:

Printed Name and Address of Witness:	Phone Number:
	Email:
	Witness' Signature:

Comments:	Record Number: 72

NOTARY RECORD

Printed Name and Address of Signer:	Phone Number:		Thumb Print:
	Email:		
	Signer's Signature:		

Service Performed:	Identification:		I.D. Number:	
O Oath	O I.D. Card	O Credible Witness		
O Acknowledgment	O Drivers License	O Known Personally	Issued By:	
O Jurat	O Passport		Issued Date:	Expiration Date:
O Other:	O Other:			

Document Type:	Date/Time Notarized:	AM PM	Document Date:	Fee Charged:

Printed Name and Address of Witness:	Phone Number:
	Email:
	Witness' Signature:

Comments:	Record Number: **73**

NOTARY RECORD

Printed Name and Address of Signer:	Phone Number:		Thumb Print:
	Email:		
	Signer's Signature:		

Service Performed:	Identification:		I.D. Number:	
O Oath	O I.D. Card	O Credible Witness		
O Acknowledgment	O Drivers License	O Known Personally	Issued By:	
O Jurat	O Passport		Issued Date:	Expiration Date:
O Other:	O Other:			

Document Type:	Date/Time Notarized:	AM PM	Document Date:	Fee Charged:

Printed Name and Address of Witness:	Phone Number:
	Email:
	Witness' Signature:

Comments:	Record Number: **74**

NOTARY RECORD

Printed Name and Address of Signer:	Phone Number:	Thumb Print:
	Email:	
	Signer's Signature:	

Service Performed:	Identification:	I.D. Number:	
O Oath	O I.D. Card O Credible Witness		
O Acknowledgment	O Drivers License O Known Personally	Issued By:	
O Jurat	O Passport	Issued Date:	Expiration Date:
O Other:	O Other:		

Document Type:	Date/Time Notarized: AM PM	Document Date:	Fee Charged:

Printed Name and Address of Witness:	Phone Number:
	Email:
	Witness' Signature:

Comments:	Record Number: **75**

NOTARY RECORD

Printed Name and Address of Signer:	Phone Number:	Thumb Print:
	Email:	
	Signer's Signature:	

Service Performed:	Identification:	I.D. Number:	
O Oath	O I.D. Card O Credible Witness		
O Acknowledgment	O Drivers License O Known Personally	Issued By:	
O Jurat	O Passport	Issued Date:	Expiration Date:
O Other:	O Other:		

Document Type:	Date/Time Notarized: AM PM	Document Date:	Fee Charged:

Printed Name and Address of Witness:	Phone Number:
	Email:
	Witness' Signature:

Comments:	Record Number: **76**

NOTARY RECORD

Printed Name and Address of Signer:	Phone Number:	Thumb Print:
	Email:	
	Signer's Signature:	

Service Performed:	Identification:	I.D. Number:	
O Oath	O I.D. Card O Credible Witness		
O Acknowledgment	O Drivers License O Known Personally	Issued By:	
O Jurat	O Passport	Issued Date:	Expiration Date:
O Other:	O Other:		

Document Type:	Date/Time Notarized: AM PM	Document Date:	Fee Charged:

Printed Name and Address of Witness:	Phone Number:
	Email:
	Witness' Signature:

Comments:	Record Number: **77**

NOTARY RECORD

Printed Name and Address of Signer:	Phone Number:	Thumb Print:
	Email:	
	Signer's Signature:	

Service Performed:	Identification:	I.D. Number:	
O Oath	O I.D. Card O Credible Witness		
O Acknowledgment	O Drivers License O Known Personally	Issued By:	
O Jurat	O Passport	Issued Date:	Expiration Date:
O Other:	O Other:		

Document Type:	Date/Time Notarized: AM PM	Document Date:	Fee Charged:

Printed Name and Address of Witness:	Phone Number:
	Email:
	Witness' Signature:

Comments:	Record Number: **78**

NOTARY RECORD

Printed Name and Address of Signer:	Phone Number:	Thumb Print:
	Email:	
	Signer's Signature:	

Service Performed:	Identification:	I.D. Number:	
O Oath	O I.D. Card O Credible Witness		
O Acknowledgment	O Drivers License O Known Personally	Issued By:	
O Jurat	O Passport	Issued Date:	Expiration Date:
O Other:	O Other:		

Document Type:	Date/Time Notarized: AM PM	Document Date:	Fee Charged:

Printed Name and Address of Witness:	Phone Number:
	Email:
	Witness' Signature:

Comments:	Record Number: 79

NOTARY RECORD

Printed Name and Address of Signer:	Phone Number:	Thumb Print:
	Email:	
	Signer's Signature:	

Service Performed:	Identification:	I.D. Number:	
O Oath	O I.D. Card O Credible Witness		
O Acknowledgment	O Drivers License O Known Personally	Issued By:	
O Jurat	O Passport	Issued Date:	Expiration Date:
O Other:	O Other:		

Document Type:	Date/Time Notarized: AM PM	Document Date:	Fee Charged:

Printed Name and Address of Witness:	Phone Number:
	Email:
	Witness' Signature:

Comments:	Record Number: 80

NOTARY RECORD

Printed Name and Address of Signer:	Phone Number:	Thumb Print:
	Email:	
	Signer's Signature:	

Service Performed:	Identification:	I.D. Number:	
O Oath	O I.D. Card O Credible Witness		
O Acknowledgment	O Drivers License O Known Personally	Issued By:	
O Jurat	O Passport	Issued Date:	Expiration Date:
O Other:	O Other:		

Document Type:	Date/Time Notarized:	AM PM	Document Date:	Fee Charged:

Printed Name and Address of Witness:	Phone Number:
	Email:
	Witness' Signature:

Comments:	Record Number: **81**

NOTARY RECORD

Printed Name and Address of Signer:	Phone Number:	Thumb Print:
	Email:	
	Signer's Signature:	

Service Performed:	Identification:	I.D. Number:	
O Oath	O I.D. Card O Credible Witness		
O Acknowledgment	O Drivers License O Known Personally	Issued By:	
O Jurat	O Passport	Issued Date:	Expiration Date:
O Other:	O Other:		

Document Type:	Date/Time Notarized:	AM PM	Document Date:	Fee Charged:

Printed Name and Address of Witness:	Phone Number:
	Email:
	Witness' Signature:

Comments:	Record Number: **82**

NOTARY RECORD

Printed Name and Address of Signer:	Phone Number:		Thumb Print:
	Email:		
	Signer's Signature:		

Service Performed:	Identification:		I.D. Number:	
O Oath	O I.D. Card	O Credible Witness		
O Acknowledgment	O Drivers License	O Known Personally	Issued By:	
O Jurat	O Passport		Issued Date:	Expiration Date:
O Other:	O Other:			

Document Type:	Date/Time Notarized:	AM PM	Document Date:	Fee Charged:

Printed Name and Address of Witness:	Phone Number:
	Email:
	Witness' Signature:

Comments:	Record Number: **83**

NOTARY RECORD

Printed Name and Address of Signer:	Phone Number:		Thumb Print:
	Email:		
	Signer's Signature:		

Service Performed:	Identification:		I.D. Number:	
O Oath	O I.D. Card	O Credible Witness		
O Acknowledgment	O Drivers License	O Known Personally	Issued By:	
O Jurat	O Passport		Issued Date:	Expiration Date:
O Other:	O Other:			

Document Type:	Date/Time Notarized:	AM PM	Document Date:	Fee Charged:

Printed Name and Address of Witness:	Phone Number:
	Email:
	Witness' Signature:

Comments:	Record Number: **84**

NOTARY RECORD

Printed Name and Address of Signer:	Phone Number:	Thumb Print:
	Email:	
	Signer's Signature:	

Service Performed:	Identification:	I.D. Number:
O Oath	O I.D. Card O Credible Witness	
O Acknowledgment	O Drivers License O Known Personally	Issued By:
O Jurat	O Passport	Issued Date: Expiration Date:
O Other:	O Other:	

Document Type:	Date/Time Notarized: AM PM	Document Date:	Fee Charged:

Printed Name and Address of Witness:	Phone Number:
	Email:
	Witness' Signature:

Comments:	Record Number: **85**

NOTARY RECORD

Printed Name and Address of Signer:	Phone Number:	Thumb Print:
	Email:	
	Signer's Signature:	

Service Performed:	Identification:	I.D. Number:
O Oath	O I.D. Card O Credible Witness	
O Acknowledgment	O Drivers License O Known Personally	Issued By:
O Jurat	O Passport	Issued Date: Expiration Date:
O Other:	O Other:	

Document Type:	Date/Time Notarized: AM PM	Document Date:	Fee Charged:

Printed Name and Address of Witness:	Phone Number:
	Email:
	Witness' Signature:

Comments:	Record Number: **86**

NOTARY RECORD

Printed Name and Address of Signer:	Phone Number:	Thumb Print:
	Email:	
	Signer's Signature:	

Service Performed:	Identification:	I.D. Number:	
O Oath	O I.D. Card O Credible Witness		
O Acknowledgment	O Drivers License O Known Personally	Issued By:	
O Jurat	O Passport		
O Other:	O Other:	Issued Date:	Expiration Date:

Document Type:	Date/Time Notarized: AM PM	Document Date:	Fee Charged:

Printed Name and Address of Witness:	Phone Number:
	Email:
	Witness' Signature:

Comments:	Record Number: **87**

NOTARY RECORD

Printed Name and Address of Signer:	Phone Number:	Thumb Print:
	Email:	
	Signer's Signature:	

Service Performed:	Identification:	I.D. Number:	
O Oath	O I.D. Card O Credible Witness		
O Acknowledgment	O Drivers License O Known Personally	Issued By:	
O Jurat	O Passport		
O Other:	O Other:	Issued Date:	Expiration Date:

Document Type:	Date/Time Notarized: AM PM	Document Date:	Fee Charged:

Printed Name and Address of Witness:	Phone Number:
	Email:
	Witness' Signature:

Comments:	Record Number: **88**

NOTARY RECORD

Printed Name and Address of Signer:	Phone Number:	Thumb Print:
	Email:	
	Signer's Signature:	

Service Performed:	Identification:	I.D. Number:	
O Oath	O I.D. Card O Credible Witness		
O Acknowledgment	O Drivers License O Known Personally	Issued By:	
O Jurat	O Passport	Issued Date:	Expiration Date:
O Other:	O Other:		

Document Type:	Date/Time Notarized: AM PM	Document Date:	Fee Charged:

Printed Name and Address of Witness:	Phone Number:
	Email:
	Witness' Signature:

Comments:	Record Number: **89**

NOTARY RECORD

Printed Name and Address of Signer:	Phone Number:	Thumb Print:
	Email:	
	Signer's Signature:	

Service Performed:	Identification:	I.D. Number:	
O Oath	O I.D. Card O Credible Witness		
O Acknowledgment	O Drivers License O Known Personally	Issued By:	
O Jurat	O Passport	Issued Date:	Expiration Date:
O Other:	O Other:		

Document Type:	Date/Time Notarized: AM PM	Document Date:	Fee Charged:

Printed Name and Address of Witness:	Phone Number:
	Email:
	Witness' Signature:

Comments:	Record Number: **90**

NOTARY RECORD

Printed Name and Address of Signer:	Phone Number:	Thumb Print:
	Email:	
	Signer's Signature:	

Service Performed:	Identification:	I.D. Number:	
O Oath	O I.D. Card　　O Credible Witness		
O Acknowledgment	O Drivers License　　O Known Personally	Issued By:	
O Jurat	O Passport	Issued Date:	Expiration Date:
O Other:	O Other:		

Document Type:	Date/Time Notarized:　　AM PM	Document Date:	Fee Charged:

Printed Name and Address of Witness:	Phone Number:
	Email:
	Witness' Signature:

Comments:	Record Number: 91

NOTARY RECORD

Printed Name and Address of Signer:	Phone Number:	Thumb Print:
	Email:	
	Signer's Signature:	

Service Performed:	Identification:	I.D. Number:	
O Oath	O I.D. Card　　O Credible Witness		
O Acknowledgment	O Drivers License　　O Known Personally	Issued By:	
O Jurat	O Passport	Issued Date:	Expiration Date:
O Other:	O Other:		

Document Type:	Date/Time Notarized:　　AM PM	Document Date:	Fee Charged:

Printed Name and Address of Witness:	Phone Number:
	Email:
	Witness' Signature:

Comments:	Record Number: 92

NOTARY RECORD

Printed Name and Address of Signer:	Phone Number:	Thumb Print:
	Email:	
	Signer's Signature:	

Service Performed:	Identification:	I.D. Number:	
O Oath	O I.D. Card O Credible Witness		
O Acknowledgment	O Drivers License O Known Personally	Issued By:	
O Jurat	O Passport		
O Other:	O Other:	Issued Date:	Expiration Date:

Document Type:	Date/Time Notarized: AM PM	Document Date:	Fee Charged:

Printed Name and Address of Witness:	Phone Number:
	Email:
	Witness' Signature:

Comments:	Record Number: 93

NOTARY RECORD

Printed Name and Address of Signer:	Phone Number:	Thumb Print:
	Email:	
	Signer's Signature:	

Service Performed:	Identification:	I.D. Number:	
O Oath	O I.D. Card O Credible Witness		
O Acknowledgment	O Drivers License O Known Personally	Issued By:	
O Jurat	O Passport		
O Other:	O Other:	Issued Date:	Expiration Date:

Document Type:	Date/Time Notarized: AM PM	Document Date:	Fee Charged:

Printed Name and Address of Witness:	Phone Number:
	Email:
	Witness' Signature:

Comments:	Record Number: 94

NOTARY RECORD

Printed Name and Address of Signer:	Phone Number:	Thumb Print:
	Email:	
	Signer's Signature:	

Service Performed:	Identification:	I.D. Number:	
O Oath	O I.D. Card O Credible Witness		
O Acknowledgment	O Drivers License O Known Personally	Issued By:	
O Jurat	O Passport	Issued Date:	Expiration Date:
O Other:	O Other:		

Document Type:	Date/Time Notarized: AM PM	Document Date:	Fee Charged:

Printed Name and Address of Witness:	Phone Number:
	Email:
	Witness' Signature:

Comments:	Record Number: 95

NOTARY RECORD

Printed Name and Address of Signer:	Phone Number:	Thumb Print:
	Email:	
	Signer's Signature:	

Service Performed:	Identification:	I.D. Number:	
O Oath	O I.D. Card O Credible Witness		
O Acknowledgment	O Drivers License O Known Personally	Issued By:	
O Jurat	O Passport	Issued Date:	Expiration Date:
O Other:	O Other:		

Document Type:	Date/Time Notarized: AM PM	Document Date:	Fee Charged:

Printed Name and Address of Witness:	Phone Number:
	Email:
	Witness' Signature:

Comments:	Record Number: 96

NOTARY RECORD

Printed Name and Address of Signer:	Phone Number:	Thumb Print:
	Email:	
	Signer's Signature:	

Service Performed:	Identification:	I.D. Number:	
O Oath	O I.D. Card O Credible Witness		
O Acknowledgment	O Drivers License O Known Personally	Issued By:	
O Jurat	O Passport	Issued Date:	Expiration Date:
O Other:	O Other:		
Document Type:	Date/Time Notarized: AM PM	Document Date:	Fee Charged:

Printed Name and Address of Witness:	Phone Number:
	Email:
	Witness' Signature:

Comments:	Record Number: **97**

NOTARY RECORD

Printed Name and Address of Signer:	Phone Number:	Thumb Print:
	Email:	
	Signer's Signature:	

Service Performed:	Identification:	I.D. Number:	
O Oath	O I.D. Card O Credible Witness		
O Acknowledgment	O Drivers License O Known Personally	Issued By:	
O Jurat	O Passport	Issued Date:	Expiration Date:
O Other:	O Other:		
Document Type:	Date/Time Notarized: AM PM	Document Date:	Fee Charged:

Printed Name and Address of Witness:	Phone Number:
	Email:
	Witness' Signature:

Comments:	Record Number: **98**

NOTARY RECORD

Printed Name and Address of Signer:	Phone Number:	Thumb Print:
	Email:	
	Signer's Signature:	

Service Performed:	Identification:	I.D. Number:	
O Oath	O I.D. Card O Credible Witness		
O Acknowledgment	O Drivers License O Known Personally	Issued By:	
O Jurat	O Passport	Issued Date:	Expiration Date:
O Other:	O Other:		

Document Type:	Date/Time Notarized: AM PM	Document Date:	Fee Charged:

Printed Name and Address of Witness:	Phone Number:
	Email:
	Witness' Signature:

Comments:	Record Number: **99**

NOTARY RECORD

Printed Name and Address of Signer:	Phone Number:	Thumb Print:
	Email:	
	Signer's Signature:	

Service Performed:	Identification:	I.D. Number:	
O Oath	O I.D. Card O Credible Witness		
O Acknowledgment	O Drivers License O Known Personally	Issued By:	
O Jurat	O Passport	Issued Date:	Expiration Date:
O Other:	O Other:		

Document Type:	Date/Time Notarized: AM PM	Document Date:	Fee Charged:

Printed Name and Address of Witness:	Phone Number:
	Email:
	Witness' Signature:

Comments:	Record Number: **100**

NOTARY RECORD

Printed Name and Address of Signer:	Phone Number:	Thumb Print:
	Email:	
	Signer's Signature:	

Service Performed:	Identification:	I.D. Number:	
O Oath	O I.D. Card O Credible Witness		
O Acknowledgment	O Drivers License O Known Personally	Issued By:	
O Jurat	O Passport		
O Other:	O Other:	Issued Date:	Expiration Date:

Document Type:	Date/Time Notarized: AM PM	Document Date:	Fee Charged:

Printed Name and Address of Witness:	Phone Number:
	Email:
	Witness' Signature:

Comments:	Record Number: **101**

NOTARY RECORD

Printed Name and Address of Signer:	Phone Number:	Thumb Print:
	Email:	
	Signer's Signature:	

Service Performed:	Identification:	I.D. Number:	
O Oath	O I.D. Card O Credible Witness		
O Acknowledgment	O Drivers License O Known Personally	Issued By:	
O Jurat	O Passport		
O Other:	O Other:	Issued Date:	Expiration Date:

Document Type:	Date/Time Notarized: AM PM	Document Date:	Fee Charged:

Printed Name and Address of Witness:	Phone Number:
	Email:
	Witness' Signature:

Comments:	Record Number: **102**

NOTARY RECORD

Printed Name and Address of Signer:	Phone Number:	Thumb Print:
	Email:	
	Signer's Signature:	

Service Performed:	Identification:	I.D. Number:	
O Oath	O I.D. Card O Credible Witness		
O Acknowledgment	O Drivers License O Known Personally	Issued By:	
O Jurat	O Passport	Issued Date:	Expiration Date:
O Other:	O Other:		
Document Type:	Date/Time Notarized: AM PM	Document Date:	Fee Charged:

Printed Name and Address of Witness:	Phone Number:
	Email:
	Witness' Signature:

Comments:	Record Number: **99**

NOTARY RECORD

Printed Name and Address of Signer:	Phone Number:	Thumb Print:
	Email:	
	Signer's Signature:	

Service Performed:	Identification:	I.D. Number:	
O Oath	O I.D. Card O Credible Witness		
O Acknowledgment	O Drivers License O Known Personally	Issued By:	
O Jurat	O Passport	Issued Date:	Expiration Date:
O Other:	O Other:		
Document Type:	Date/Time Notarized: AM PM	Document Date:	Fee Charged:

Printed Name and Address of Witness:	Phone Number:
	Email:
	Witness' Signature:

Comments:	Record Number: **100**

NOTARY RECORD

Printed Name and Address of Signer:	Phone Number:	Thumb Print:
	Email:	
	Signer's Signature:	

Service Performed:	Identification:	I.D. Number:	
O Oath	O I.D. Card O Credible Witness		
O Acknowledgment	O Drivers License O Known Personally	Issued By:	
O Jurat	O Passport	Issued Date:	Expiration Date:
O Other:	O Other:		

Document Type:	Date/Time Notarized: AM PM	Document Date:	Fee Charged:

Printed Name and Address of Witness:	Phone Number:
	Email:
	Witness' Signature:

Comments:	Record Number: **101**

NOTARY RECORD

Printed Name and Address of Signer:	Phone Number:	Thumb Print:
	Email:	
	Signer's Signature:	

Service Performed:	Identification:	I.D. Number:	
O Oath	O I.D. Card O Credible Witness		
O Acknowledgment	O Drivers License O Known Personally	Issued By:	
O Jurat	O Passport	Issued Date:	Expiration Date:
O Other:	O Other:		

Document Type:	Date/Time Notarized: AM PM	Document Date:	Fee Charged:

Printed Name and Address of Witness:	Phone Number:
	Email:
	Witness' Signature:

Comments:	Record Number: **102**

NOTARY RECORD

Printed Name and Address of Signer:	Phone Number:		Thumb Print:
	Email:		
	Signer's Signature:		

Service Performed:	Identification:		I.D. Number:	
O Oath	O I.D. Card	O Credible Witness		
O Acknowledgment	O Drivers License	O Known Personally	Issued By:	
O Jurat	O Passport		Issued Date:	Expiration Date:
O Other:	O Other:			

Document Type:	Date/Time Notarized: AM PM	Document Date:	Fee Charged:

Printed Name and Address of Witness:	Phone Number:
	Email:
	Witness' Signature:

Comments:	Record Number: **103**

NOTARY RECORD

Printed Name and Address of Signer:	Phone Number:		Thumb Print:
	Email:		
	Signer's Signature:		

Service Performed:	Identification:		I.D. Number:	
O Oath	O I.D. Card	O Credible Witness		
O Acknowledgment	O Drivers License	O Known Personally	Issued By:	
O Jurat	O Passport		Issued Date:	Expiration Date:
O Other:	O Other:			

Document Type:	Date/Time Notarized: AM PM	Document Date:	Fee Charged:

Printed Name and Address of Witness:	Phone Number:
	Email:
	Witness' Signature:

Comments:	Record Number: **104**

NOTARY RECORD

Printed Name and Address of Signer:	Phone Number:	Thumb Print:
	Email:	
	Signer's Signature:	

Service Performed:	Identification:	I.D. Number:	
O Oath	O I.D. Card O Credible Witness		
O Acknowledgment	O Drivers License O Known Personally	Issued By:	
O Jurat	O Passport	Issued Date:	Expiration Date:
O Other:	O Other:		

Document Type:	Date/Time Notarized: AM PM	Document Date:	Fee Charged:

Printed Name and Address of Witness:	Phone Number:
	Email:
	Witness' Signature:

Comments:	Record Number: 105

NOTARY RECORD

Printed Name and Address of Signer:	Phone Number:	Thumb Print:
	Email:	
	Signer's Signature:	

Service Performed:	Identification:	I.D. Number:	
O Oath	O I.D. Card O Credible Witness		
O Acknowledgment	O Drivers License O Known Personally	Issued By:	
O Jurat	O Passport	Issued Date:	Expiration Date:
O Other:	O Other:		

Document Type:	Date/Time Notarized: AM PM	Document Date:	Fee Charged:

Printed Name and Address of Witness:	Phone Number:
	Email:
	Witness' Signature:

Comments:	Record Number: 106

NOTARY RECORD

Printed Name and Address of Signer:

Phone Number:

Email:

Signer's Signature:

Thumb Print:

Service Performed:
- O Oath
- O Acknowledgment
- O Jurat
- O Other:

Identification:
- O I.D. Card
- O Drivers License
- O Passport
- O Other:
- O Credible Witness
- O Known Personally

I.D. Number:

Issued By:

Issued Date:

Expiration Date:

Document Type:

Date/Time Notarized: AM PM

Document Date:

Fee Charged:

Printed Name and Address of Witness:

Phone Number:

Email:

Witness' Signature:

Comments:

Record Number:

107

NOTARY RECORD

Printed Name and Address of Signer:

Phone Number:

Email:

Signer's Signature:

Thumb Print:

Service Performed:
- O Oath
- O Acknowledgment
- O Jurat
- O Other:

Identification:
- O I.D. Card
- O Drivers License
- O Passport
- O Other:
- O Credible Witness
- O Known Personally

I.D. Number:

Issued By:

Issued Date:

Expiration Date:

Document Type:

Date/Time Notarized: AM PM

Document Date:

Fee Charged:

Printed Name and Address of Witness:

Phone Number:

Email:

Witness' Signature:

Comments:

Record Number:

108

NOTARY RECORD

Printed Name and Address of Signer:	Phone Number:	Thumb Print:
	Email:	
	Signer's Signature:	

Service Performed:	Identification:	I.D. Number:	
O Oath	O I.D. Card O Credible Witness		
O Acknowledgment	O Drivers License O Known Personally	Issued By:	
O Jurat	O Passport		
O Other:	O Other:	Issued Date:	Expiration Date:

Document Type:	Date/Time Notarized: AM PM	Document Date:	Fee Charged:

Printed Name and Address of Witness:	Phone Number:
	Email:
	Witness' Signature:

Comments:	Record Number:
	109

NOTARY RECORD

Printed Name and Address of Signer:	Phone Number:	Thumb Print:
	Email:	
	Signer's Signature:	

Service Performed:	Identification:	I.D. Number:	
O Oath	O I.D. Card O Credible Witness		
O Acknowledgment	O Drivers License O Known Personally	Issued By:	
O Jurat	O Passport		
O Other:	O Other:	Issued Date:	Expiration Date:

Document Type:	Date/Time Notarized: AM PM	Document Date:	Fee Charged:

Printed Name and Address of Witness:	Phone Number:
	Email:
	Witness' Signature:

Comments:	Record Number:
	110

NOTARY RECORD

Printed Name and Address of Signer:	Phone Number:	Thumb Print:
	Email:	
	Signer's Signature:	

Service Performed:	Identification:	I.D. Number:	
O Oath	O I.D. Card O Credible Witness		
O Acknowledgment	O Drivers License O Known Personally	Issued By:	
O Jurat	O Passport	Issued Date:	Expiration Date:
O Other:	O Other:		

Document Type:	Date/Time Notarized: AM PM	Document Date:	Fee Charged:

Printed Name and Address of Witness:	Phone Number:
	Email:
	Witness' Signature:

Comments:	Record Number: **111**

NOTARY RECORD

Printed Name and Address of Signer:	Phone Number:	Thumb Print:
	Email:	
	Signer's Signature:	

Service Performed:	Identification:	I.D. Number:	
O Oath	O I.D. Card O Credible Witness		
O Acknowledgment	O Drivers License O Known Personally	Issued By:	
O Jurat	O Passport	Issued Date:	Expiration Date:
O Other:	O Other:		

Document Type:	Date/Time Notarized: AM PM	Document Date:	Fee Charged:

Printed Name and Address of Witness:	Phone Number:
	Email:
	Witness' Signature:

Comments:	Record Number: **112**

NOTARY RECORD

Printed Name and Address of Signer:	Phone Number:	Thumb Print:
	Email:	
	Signer's Signature:	

Service Performed:	Identification:	I.D. Number:	
O Oath	O I.D. Card O Credible Witness		
O Acknowledgment	O Drivers License O Known Personally	Issued By:	
O Jurat	O Passport	Issued Date:	Expiration Date:
O Other:	O Other:		

Document Type:	Date/Time Notarized:	AM PM	Document Date:	Fee Charged:

Printed Name and Address of Witness:	Phone Number:
	Email:
	Witness' Signature:

Comments:	Record Number: **113**

NOTARY RECORD

Printed Name and Address of Signer:	Phone Number:	Thumb Print:
	Email:	
	Signer's Signature:	

Service Performed:	Identification:	I.D. Number:	
O Oath	O I.D. Card O Credible Witness		
O Acknowledgment	O Drivers License O Known Personally	Issued By:	
O Jurat	O Passport	Issued Date:	Expiration Date:
O Other:	O Other:		

Document Type:	Date/Time Notarized:	AM PM	Document Date:	Fee Charged:

Printed Name and Address of Witness:	Phone Number:
	Email:
	Witness' Signature:

Comments:	Record Number: **114**

NOTARY RECORD

Printed Name and Address of Signer:

Phone Number:

Email:

Signer's Signature:

Thumb Print:

Service Performed:	Identification:		I.D. Number:	
O Oath	O I.D. Card	O Credible Witness		
O Acknowledgment	O Drivers License	O Known Personally	**Issued By:**	
O Jurat	O Passport		**Issued Date:**	**Expiration Date:**
O Other:	O Other:			

Document Type:	Date/Time Notarized: AM PM	Document Date:	Fee Charged:

Printed Name and Address of Witness:

Phone Number:

Email:

Witness' Signature:

Comments:

Record Number:

115

NOTARY RECORD

Printed Name and Address of Signer:

Phone Number:

Email:

Signer's Signature:

Thumb Print:

Service Performed:	Identification:		I.D. Number:	
O Oath	O I.D. Card	O Credible Witness		
O Acknowledgment	O Drivers License	O Known Personally	**Issued By:**	
O Jurat	O Passport		**Issued Date:**	**Expiration Date:**
O Other:	O Other:			

Document Type:	Date/Time Notarized: AM PM	Document Date:	Fee Charged:

Printed Name and Address of Witness:

Phone Number:

Email:

Witness' Signature:

Comments:

Record Number:

116

NOTARY RECORD

Printed Name and Address of Signer:

Phone Number:

Email:

Signer's Signature:

Thumb Print:

Service Performed:	Identification:		I.D. Number:	
O Oath	O I.D. Card	O Credible Witness		
O Acknowledgment	O Drivers License	O Known Personally	**Issued By:**	
O Jurat	O Passport		**Issued Date:**	**Expiration Date:**
O Other:	O Other:			

Document Type:	Date/Time Notarized:	AM PM	Document Date:	Fee Charged:

Printed Name and Address of Witness:

Phone Number:

Email:

Witness' Signature:

Comments:	Record Number:
	117

NOTARY RECORD

Printed Name and Address of Signer:

Phone Number:

Email:

Signer's Signature:

Thumb Print:

Service Performed:	Identification:		I.D. Number:	
O Oath	O I.D. Card	O Credible Witness		
O Acknowledgment	O Drivers License	O Known Personally	**Issued By:**	
O Jurat	O Passport		**Issued Date:**	**Expiration Date:**
O Other:	O Other:			

Document Type:	Date/Time Notarized:	AM PM	Document Date:	Fee Charged:

Printed Name and Address of Witness:

Phone Number:

Email:

Witness' Signature:

Comments:	Record Number:
	118

NOTARY RECORD

Printed Name and Address of Signer:	Phone Number:	Thumb Print:
	Email:	
	Signer's Signature:	

Service Performed:	Identification:	I.D. Number:	
O Oath	O I.D. Card O Credible Witness		
O Acknowledgment	O Drivers License O Known Personally	Issued By:	
O Jurat	O Passport	Issued Date:	Expiration Date:
O Other:	O Other:		

Document Type:	Date/Time Notarized: AM PM	Document Date:	Fee Charged:

Printed Name and Address of Witness:	Phone Number:
	Email:
	Witness' Signature:

Comments:	Record Number: **119**

NOTARY RECORD

Printed Name and Address of Signer:	Phone Number:	Thumb Print:
	Email:	
	Signer's Signature:	

Service Performed:	Identification:	I.D. Number:	
O Oath	O I.D. Card O Credible Witness		
O Acknowledgment	O Drivers License O Known Personally	Issued By:	
O Jurat	O Passport	Issued Date:	Expiration Date:
O Other:	O Other:		

Document Type:	Date/Time Notarized: AM PM	Document Date:	Fee Charged:

Printed Name and Address of Witness:	Phone Number:
	Email:
	Witness' Signature:

Comments:	Record Number: **120**

NOTARY RECORD

Printed Name and Address of Signer:

Phone Number:

Email:

Signer's Signature:

Thumb Print:

Service Performed:	Identification:		I.D. Number:	
O Oath	O I.D. Card	O Credible Witness		
O Acknowledgment	O Drivers License	O Known Personally	**Issued By:**	
O Jurat	O Passport		**Issued Date:**	**Expiration Date:**
O Other:	O Other:			

Document Type:	Date/Time Notarized:	AM PM	Document Date:	Fee Charged:

Printed Name and Address of Witness:

Phone Number:

Email:

Witness' Signature:

Comments:

Record Number:

121

NOTARY RECORD

Printed Name and Address of Signer:

Phone Number:

Email:

Signer's Signature:

Thumb Print:

Service Performed:	Identification:		I.D. Number:	
O Oath	O I.D. Card	O Credible Witness		
O Acknowledgment	O Drivers License	O Known Personally	**Issued By:**	
O Jurat	O Passport		**Issued Date:**	**Expiration Date:**
O Other:	O Other:			

Document Type:	Date/Time Notarized:	AM PM	Document Date:	Fee Charged:

Printed Name and Address of Witness:

Phone Number:

Email:

Witness' Signature:

Comments:

Record Number:

122

NOTARY RECORD

Printed Name and Address of Signer:	Phone Number:	Thumb Print:
	Email:	
	Signer's Signature:	

Service Performed:	Identification:	I.D. Number:	
O Oath	O I.D. Card　　O Credible Witness		
O Acknowledgment	O Drivers License　O Known Personally	Issued By:	
O Jurat	O Passport	Issued Date:	Expiration Date:
O Other:	O Other:		

Document Type:	Date/Time Notarized:　　AM　PM	Document Date:	Fee Charged:

Printed Name and Address of Witness:	Phone Number:
	Email:
	Witness' Signature:

Comments:	Record Number: **123**

NOTARY RECORD

Printed Name and Address of Signer:	Phone Number:	Thumb Print:
	Email:	
	Signer's Signature:	

Service Performed:	Identification:	I.D. Number:	
O Oath	O I.D. Card　　O Credible Witness		
O Acknowledgment	O Drivers License　O Known Personally	Issued By:	
O Jurat	O Passport	Issued Date:	Expiration Date:
O Other:	O Other:		

Document Type:	Date/Time Notarized:　　AM　PM	Document Date:	Fee Charged:

Printed Name and Address of Witness:	Phone Number:
	Email:
	Witness' Signature:

Comments:	Record Number: **124**

NOTARY RECORD

Printed Name and Address of Signer:

Phone Number:

Email:

Signer's Signature:

Thumb Print:

Service Performed:	Identification:		I.D. Number:	
O Oath	O I.D. Card	O Credible Witness		
O Acknowledgment	O Drivers License	O Known Personally	**Issued By:**	
O Jurat	O Passport		**Issued Date:**	**Expiration Date:**
O Other:	O Other:			

Document Type:	Date/Time Notarized:	AM PM	Document Date:	Fee Charged:

Printed Name and Address of Witness:

Phone Number:

Email:

Witness' Signature:

Comments:

Record Number:
125

NOTARY RECORD

Printed Name and Address of Signer:

Phone Number:

Email:

Signer's Signature:

Thumb Print:

Service Performed:	Identification:		I.D. Number:	
O Oath	O I.D. Card	O Credible Witness		
O Acknowledgment	O Drivers License	O Known Personally	**Issued By:**	
O Jurat	O Passport		**Issued Date:**	**Expiration Date:**
O Other:	O Other:			

Document Type:	Date/Time Notarized:	AM PM	Document Date:	Fee Charged:

Printed Name and Address of Witness:

Phone Number:

Email:

Witness' Signature:

Comments:

Record Number:
126

NOTARY RECORD

Printed Name and Address of Signer:	Phone Number:	Thumb Print:
	Email:	
	Signer's Signature:	

Service Performed:	Identification:	I.D. Number:	
O Oath	O I.D. Card O Credible Witness		
O Acknowledgment	O Drivers License O Known Personally	Issued By:	
O Jurat	O Passport		
O Other:	O Other:	Issued Date:	Expiration Date:

Document Type:	Date/Time Notarized: AM PM	Document Date:	Fee Charged:

Printed Name and Address of Witness:	Phone Number:
	Email:
	Witness' Signature:

Comments:	Record Number: 127

NOTARY RECORD

Printed Name and Address of Signer:	Phone Number:	Thumb Print:
	Email:	
	Signer's Signature:	

Service Performed:	Identification:	I.D. Number:	
O Oath	O I.D. Card O Credible Witness		
O Acknowledgment	O Drivers License O Known Personally	Issued By:	
O Jurat	O Passport		
O Other:	O Other:	Issued Date:	Expiration Date:

Document Type:	Date/Time Notarized: AM PM	Document Date:	Fee Charged:

Printed Name and Address of Witness:	Phone Number:
	Email:
	Witness' Signature:

Comments:	Record Number: 128

NOTARY RECORD

Printed Name and Address of Signer:

Phone Number:

Email:

Signer's Signature:

Thumb Print:

Service Performed:

O Oath

O Acknowledgment

O Jurat

O Other:

Identification:

O I.D. Card

O Drivers License

O Passport

O Other:

O Credible Witness

O Known Personally

I.D. Number:

Issued By:

Issued Date:

Expiration Date:

Document Type:

Date/Time Notarized: AM PM

Document Date:

Fee Charged:

Printed Name and Address of Witness:

Phone Number:

Email:

Witness' Signature:

Comments:

Record Number:

129

NOTARY RECORD

Printed Name and Address of Signer:

Phone Number:

Email:

Signer's Signature:

Thumb Print:

Service Performed:

O Oath

O Acknowledgment

O Jurat

O Other:

Identification:

O I.D. Card

O Drivers License

O Passport

O Other:

O Credible Witness

O Known Personally

I.D. Number:

Issued By:

Issued Date:

Expiration Date:

Document Type:

Date/Time Notarized: AM PM

Document Date:

Fee Charged:

Printed Name and Address of Witness:

Phone Number:

Email:

Witness' Signature:

Comments:

Record Number:

130

NOTARY RECORD

Printed Name and Address of Signer:	Phone Number:	Thumb Print:
	Email:	
	Signer's Signature:	

Service Performed:	Identification:	I.D. Number:	
O Oath	O I.D. Card O Credible Witness		
O Acknowledgment	O Drivers License O Known Personally	Issued By:	
O Jurat	O Passport	Issued Date:	Expiration Date:
O Other:	O Other:		

Document Type:	Date/Time Notarized: AM PM	Document Date:	Fee Charged:

Printed Name and Address of Witness:	Phone Number:
	Email:
	Witness' Signature:

Comments:	Record Number:
	131

NOTARY RECORD

Printed Name and Address of Signer:	Phone Number:	Thumb Print:
	Email:	
	Signer's Signature:	

Service Performed:	Identification:	I.D. Number:	
O Oath	O I.D. Card O Credible Witness		
O Acknowledgment	O Drivers License O Known Personally	Issued By:	
O Jurat	O Passport	Issued Date:	Expiration Date:
O Other:	O Other:		

Document Type:	Date/Time Notarized: AM PM	Document Date:	Fee Charged:

Printed Name and Address of Witness:	Phone Number:
	Email:
	Witness' Signature:

Comments:	Record Number:
	132

NOTARY RECORD

Printed Name and Address of Signer:	Phone Number:	Thumb Print:
	Email:	
	Signer's Signature:	

Service Performed:	Identification:	I.D. Number:	
O Oath	O I.D. Card O Credible Witness		
O Acknowledgment	O Drivers License O Known Personally	Issued By:	
O Jurat	O Passport		
O Other:	O Other:	Issued Date:	Expiration Date:

Document Type:	Date/Time Notarized: AM PM	Document Date:	Fee Charged:

Printed Name and Address of Witness:	Phone Number:
	Email:
	Witness' Signature:

Comments:	Record Number:
	133

NOTARY RECORD

Printed Name and Address of Signer:	Phone Number:	Thumb Print:
	Email:	
	Signer's Signature:	

Service Performed:	Identification:	I.D. Number:	
O Oath	O I.D. Card O Credible Witness		
O Acknowledgment	O Drivers License O Known Personally	Issued By:	
O Jurat	O Passport		
O Other:	O Other:	Issued Date:	Expiration Date:

Document Type:	Date/Time Notarized: AM PM	Document Date:	Fee Charged:

Printed Name and Address of Witness:	Phone Number:
	Email:
	Witness' Signature:

Comments:	Record Number:
	134

NOTARY RECORD

Printed Name and Address of Signer:	Phone Number:	Thumb Print:
	Email:	
	Signer's Signature:	

Service Performed:	Identification:	I.D. Number:	
O Oath	O I.D. Card O Credible Witness		
O Acknowledgment	O Drivers License O Known Personally	Issued By:	
O Jurat	O Passport	Issued Date:	Expiration Date:
O Other:	O Other:		

Document Type:	Date/Time Notarized: AM PM	Document Date:	Fee Charged:

Printed Name and Address of Witness:	Phone Number:
	Email:
	Witness' Signature:

Comments:	Record Number: **135**

NOTARY RECORD

Printed Name and Address of Signer:	Phone Number:	Thumb Print:
	Email:	
	Signer's Signature:	

Service Performed:	Identification:	I.D. Number:	
O Oath	O I.D. Card O Credible Witness		
O Acknowledgment	O Drivers License O Known Personally	Issued By:	
O Jurat	O Passport	Issued Date:	Expiration Date:
O Other:	O Other:		

Document Type:	Date/Time Notarized: AM PM	Document Date:	Fee Charged:

Printed Name and Address of Witness:	Phone Number:
	Email:
	Witness' Signature:

Comments:	Record Number: **136**

NOTARY RECORD

Printed Name and Address of Signer:

Phone Number:

Email:

Signer's Signature:

Thumb Print:

Service Performed:
- O Oath
- O Acknowledgment
- O Jurat
- O Other:

Identification:
- O I.D. Card
- O Drivers License
- O Passport
- O Other:
- O Credible Witness
- O Known Personally

I.D. Number:

Issued By:

Issued Date:

Expiration Date:

Document Type:

Date/Time Notarized: AM / PM

Document Date:

Fee Charged:

Printed Name and Address of Witness:

Phone Number:

Email:

Witness' Signature:

Comments:

Record Number:

137

NOTARY RECORD

Printed Name and Address of Signer:

Phone Number:

Email:

Signer's Signature:

Thumb Print:

Service Performed:
- O Oath
- O Acknowledgment
- O Jurat
- O Other:

Identification:
- O I.D. Card
- O Drivers License
- O Passport
- O Other:
- O Credible Witness
- O Known Personally

I.D. Number:

Issued By:

Issued Date:

Expiration Date:

Document Type:

Date/Time Notarized: AM / PM

Document Date:

Fee Charged:

Printed Name and Address of Witness:

Phone Number:

Email:

Witness' Signature:

Comments:

Record Number:

138

NOTARY RECORD

Printed Name and Address of Signer:	Phone Number:	Thumb Print:
	Email:	
	Signer's Signature:	

Service Performed:	Identification:	I.D. Number:	
O Oath	O I.D. Card O Credible Witness		
O Acknowledgment	O Drivers License O Known Personally	Issued By:	
O Jurat	O Passport	Issued Date:	Expiration Date:
O Other:	O Other:		

Document Type:	Date/Time Notarized: AM PM	Document Date:	Fee Charged:

Printed Name and Address of Witness:	Phone Number:
	Email:
	Witness' Signature:

Comments:	Record Number: 139

NOTARY RECORD

Printed Name and Address of Signer:	Phone Number:	Thumb Print:
	Email:	
	Signer's Signature:	

Service Performed:	Identification:	I.D. Number:	
O Oath	O I.D. Card O Credible Witness		
O Acknowledgment	O Drivers License O Known Personally	Issued By:	
O Jurat	O Passport	Issued Date:	Expiration Date:
O Other:	O Other:		

Document Type:	Date/Time Notarized: AM PM	Document Date:	Fee Charged:

Printed Name and Address of Witness:	Phone Number:
	Email:
	Witness' Signature:

Comments:	Record Number: 140

NOTARY RECORD

Printed Name and Address of Signer:

Phone Number:

Email:

Signer's Signature:

Thumb Print:

Service Performed:
- ○ Oath
- ○ Acknowledgment
- ○ Jurat
- ○ Other:

Identification:
- ○ I.D. Card   ○ Credible Witness
- ○ Drivers License   ○ Known Personally
- ○ Passport
- ○ Other:

I.D. Number:

Issued By:

Issued Date:

Expiration Date:

Document Type:

Date/Time Notarized: AM PM

Document Date:

Fee Charged:

Printed Name and Address of Witness:

Phone Number:

Email:

Witness' Signature:

Comments:

Record Number:
141

NOTARY RECORD

Printed Name and Address of Signer:

Phone Number:

Email:

Signer's Signature:

Thumb Print:

Service Performed:
- ○ Oath
- ○ Acknowledgment
- ○ Jurat
- ○ Other:

Identification:
- ○ I.D. Card   ○ Credible Witness
- ○ Drivers License   ○ Known Personally
- ○ Passport
- ○ Other:

I.D. Number:

Issued By:

Issued Date:

Expiration Date:

Document Type:

Date/Time Notarized: AM PM

Document Date:

Fee Charged:

Printed Name and Address of Witness:

Phone Number:

Email:

Witness' Signature:

Comments:

Record Number:
142

NOTARY RECORD

Printed Name and Address of Signer:	Phone Number:	Thumb Print:
	Email:	
	Signer's Signature:	

Service Performed:	Identification:	I.D. Number:	
O Oath	O I.D. Card O Credible Witness		
O Acknowledgment	O Drivers License O Known Personally	Issued By:	
O Jurat	O Passport	Issued Date:	Expiration Date:
O Other:	O Other:		

Document Type:	Date/Time Notarized: AM PM	Document Date:	Fee Charged:

Printed Name and Address of Witness:	Phone Number:
	Email:
	Witness' Signature:

Comments:	Record Number: **143**

NOTARY RECORD

Printed Name and Address of Signer:	Phone Number:	Thumb Print:
	Email:	
	Signer's Signature:	

Service Performed:	Identification:	I.D. Number:	
O Oath	O I.D. Card O Credible Witness		
O Acknowledgment	O Drivers License O Known Personally	Issued By:	
O Jurat	O Passport	Issued Date:	Expiration Date:
O Other:	O Other:		

Document Type:	Date/Time Notarized: AM PM	Document Date:	Fee Charged:

Printed Name and Address of Witness:	Phone Number:
	Email:
	Witness' Signature:

Comments:	Record Number: **144**

NOTARY RECORD

Printed Name and Address of Signer:

Phone Number:

Email:

Signer's Signature:

Thumb Print:

Service Performed:
- O Oath
- O Acknowledgment
- O Jurat
- O Other:

Identification:
- O I.D. Card
- O Drivers License
- O Passport
- O Other:
- O Credible Witness
- O Known Personally

I.D. Number:

Issued By:

Issued Date:

Expiration Date:

Document Type:

Date/Time Notarized: AM PM

Document Date:

Fee Charged:

Printed Name and Address of Witness:

Phone Number:

Email:

Witness' Signature:

Comments:

Record Number:
145

NOTARY RECORD

Printed Name and Address of Signer:

Phone Number:

Email:

Signer's Signature:

Thumb Print:

Service Performed:
- O Oath
- O Acknowledgment
- O Jurat
- O Other:

Identification:
- O I.D. Card
- O Drivers License
- O Passport
- O Other:
- O Credible Witness
- O Known Personally

I.D. Number:

Issued By:

Issued Date:

Expiration Date:

Document Type:

Date/Time Notarized: AM PM

Document Date:

Fee Charged:

Printed Name and Address of Witness:

Phone Number:

Email:

Witness' Signature:

Comments:

Record Number:
146

NOTARY RECORD

Printed Name and Address of Signer:	Phone Number:	Thumb Print:
	Email:	
	Signer's Signature:	

Service Performed:	Identification:	I.D. Number:	
O Oath	O I.D. Card O Credible Witness		
O Acknowledgment	O Drivers License O Known Personally	Issued By:	
O Jurat	O Passport	Issued Date:	Expiration Date:
O Other:	O Other:		

Document Type:	Date/Time Notarized: AM PM	Document Date:	Fee Charged:

Printed Name and Address of Witness:	Phone Number:
	Email:
	Witness' Signature:

Comments:	Record Number: **147**

NOTARY RECORD

Printed Name and Address of Signer:	Phone Number:	Thumb Print:
	Email:	
	Signer's Signature:	

Service Performed:	Identification:	I.D. Number:	
O Oath	O I.D. Card O Credible Witness		
O Acknowledgment	O Drivers License O Known Personally	Issued By:	
O Jurat	O Passport	Issued Date:	Expiration Date:
O Other:	O Other:		

Document Type:	Date/Time Notarized: AM PM	Document Date:	Fee Charged:

Printed Name and Address of Witness:	Phone Number:
	Email:
	Witness' Signature:

Comments:	Record Number: **148**

NOTARY RECORD

Printed Name and Address of Signer:	Phone Number:	Thumb Print:
	Email:	
	Signer's Signature:	

Service Performed:	Identification:	I.D. Number:	
O Oath	O I.D. Card O Credible Witness		
O Acknowledgment	O Drivers License O Known Personally	Issued By:	
O Jurat	O Passport	Issued Date:	Expiration Date:
O Other:	O Other:		

Document Type:	Date/Time Notarized: AM PM	Document Date:	Fee Charged:

Printed Name and Address of Witness:	Phone Number:
	Email:
	Witness' Signature:

Comments:	Record Number: 149

NOTARY RECORD

Printed Name and Address of Signer:	Phone Number:	Thumb Print:
	Email:	
	Signer's Signature:	

Service Performed:	Identification:	I.D. Number:	
O Oath	O I.D. Card O Credible Witness		
O Acknowledgment	O Drivers License O Known Personally	Issued By:	
O Jurat	O Passport	Issued Date:	Expiration Date:
O Other:	O Other:		

Document Type:	Date/Time Notarized: AM PM	Document Date:	Fee Charged:

Printed Name and Address of Witness:	Phone Number:
	Email:
	Witness' Signature:

Comments:	Record Number: 150

NOTARY RECORD

Printed Name and Address of Signer:

Phone Number:

Email:

Signer's Signature:

Thumb Print:

Service Performed:	Identification:		I.D. Number:
O Oath	O I.D. Card	O Credible Witness	
O Acknowledgment	O Drivers License	O Known Personally	**Issued By:**
O Jurat	O Passport		
O Other:	O Other:		**Issued Date:** / **Expiration Date:**

Document Type:	Date/Time Notarized:	AM PM	Document Date:	Fee Charged:

Printed Name and Address of Witness:

Phone Number:

Email:

Witness' Signature:

Comments:

Record Number:

151

NOTARY RECORD

Printed Name and Address of Signer:

Phone Number:

Email:

Signer's Signature:

Thumb Print:

Service Performed:	Identification:		I.D. Number:
O Oath	O I.D. Card	O Credible Witness	
O Acknowledgment	O Drivers License	O Known Personally	**Issued By:**
O Jurat	O Passport		
O Other:	O Other:		**Issued Date:** / **Expiration Date:**

Document Type:	Date/Time Notarized:	AM PM	Document Date:	Fee Charged:

Printed Name and Address of Witness:

Phone Number:

Email:

Witness' Signature:

Comments:

Record Number:

152

NOTARY RECORD

Printed Name and Address of Signer:

Phone Number:

Email:

Signer's Signature:

Thumb Print:

Service Performed:
- O Oath
- O Acknowledgment
- O Jurat
- O Other:

Identification:
- O I.D. Card
- O Drivers License
- O Passport
- O Other:
- O Credible Witness
- O Known Personally

I.D. Number:

Issued By:

Issued Date:

Expiration Date:

Document Type:

Date/Time Notarized: AM PM

Document Date:

Fee Charged:

Printed Name and Address of Witness:

Phone Number:

Email:

Witness' Signature:

Comments:

Record Number:
153

NOTARY RECORD

Printed Name and Address of Signer:

Phone Number:

Email:

Signer's Signature:

Thumb Print:

Service Performed:
- O Oath
- O Acknowledgment
- O Jurat
- O Other:

Identification:
- O I.D. Card
- O Drivers License
- O Passport
- O Other:
- O Credible Witness
- O Known Personally

I.D. Number:

Issued By:

Issued Date:

Expiration Date:

Document Type:

Date/Time Notarized: AM PM

Document Date:

Fee Charged:

Printed Name and Address of Witness:

Phone Number:

Email:

Witness' Signature:

Comments:

Record Number:
154

NOTARY RECORD

Printed Name and Address of Signer:

Phone Number:

Email:

Signer's Signature:

Thumb Print:

Service Performed:	Identification:		I.D. Number:	
O Oath	O I.D. Card	O Credible Witness		
O Acknowledgment	O Drivers License	O Known Personally	**Issued By:**	
O Jurat	O Passport		**Issued Date:**	**Expiration Date:**
O Other:	O Other:			

Document Type:	Date/Time Notarized:	AM PM	Document Date:	Fee Charged:

Printed Name and Address of Witness:

Phone Number:

Email:

Witness' Signature:

Comments:	Record Number: **155**

NOTARY RECORD

Printed Name and Address of Signer:

Phone Number:

Email:

Signer's Signature:

Thumb Print:

Service Performed:	Identification:		I.D. Number:	
O Oath	O I.D. Card	O Credible Witness		
O Acknowledgment	O Drivers License	O Known Personally	**Issued By:**	
O Jurat	O Passport		**Issued Date:**	**Expiration Date:**
O Other:	O Other:			

Document Type:	Date/Time Notarized:	AM PM	Document Date:	Fee Charged:

Printed Name and Address of Witness:

Phone Number:

Email:

Witness' Signature:

Comments:	Record Number: **156**

NOTARY RECORD

Printed Name and Address of Signer:	Phone Number:	Thumb Print:
	Email:	
	Signer's Signature:	

Service Performed:	Identification:	I.D. Number:	
O Oath	O I.D. Card O Credible Witness		
O Acknowledgment	O Drivers License O Known Personally	Issued By:	
O Jurat	O Passport		
O Other:	O Other:	Issued Date:	Expiration Date:

Document Type:	Date/Time Notarized: AM PM	Document Date:	Fee Charged:

Printed Name and Address of Witness:	Phone Number:
	Email:
	Witness' Signature:

Comments:	Record Number: **157**

NOTARY RECORD

Printed Name and Address of Signer:	Phone Number:	Thumb Print:
	Email:	
	Signer's Signature:	

Service Performed:	Identification:	I.D. Number:	
O Oath	O I.D. Card O Credible Witness		
O Acknowledgment	O Drivers License O Known Personally	Issued By:	
O Jurat	O Passport		
O Other:	O Other:	Issued Date:	Expiration Date:

Document Type:	Date/Time Notarized: AM PM	Document Date:	Fee Charged:

Printed Name and Address of Witness:	Phone Number:
	Email:
	Witness' Signature:

Comments:	Record Number: **158**

NOTARY RECORD

Printed Name and Address of Signer:	Phone Number:		Thumb Print:
	Email:		
	Signer's Signature:		

Service Performed:	Identification:		I.D. Number:	
O Oath	O I.D. Card	O Credible Witness		
O Acknowledgment	O Drivers License	O Known Personally	Issued By:	
O Jurat	O Passport			
O Other:	O Other:		Issued Date:	Expiration Date:

Document Type:	Date/Time Notarized:	AM PM	Document Date:	Fee Charged:

Printed Name and Address of Witness:	Phone Number:
	Email:
	Witness' Signature:

Comments:	Record Number:
	159

NOTARY RECORD

Printed Name and Address of Signer:	Phone Number:		Thumb Print:
	Email:		
	Signer's Signature:		

Service Performed:	Identification:		I.D. Number:	
O Oath	O I.D. Card	O Credible Witness		
O Acknowledgment	O Drivers License	O Known Personally	Issued By:	
O Jurat	O Passport			
O Other:	O Other:		Issued Date:	Expiration Date:

Document Type:	Date/Time Notarized:	AM PM	Document Date:	Fee Charged:

Printed Name and Address of Witness:	Phone Number:
	Email:
	Witness' Signature:

Comments:	Record Number:
	160

NOTARY RECORD

Printed Name and Address of Signer:

Phone Number:

Email:

Signer's Signature:

Thumb Print:

Service Performed:
- O Oath
- O Acknowledgment
- O Jurat
- O Other:

Identification:
- O I.D. Card
- O Drivers License
- O Passport
- O Other:
- O Credible Witness
- O Known Personally

I.D. Number:

Issued By:

Issued Date:

Expiration Date:

Document Type:

Date/Time Notarized: AM PM

Document Date:

Fee Charged:

Printed Name and Address of Witness:

Phone Number:

Email:

Witness' Signature:

Comments:

Record Number:
161

NOTARY RECORD

Printed Name and Address of Signer:

Phone Number:

Email:

Signer's Signature:

Thumb Print:

Service Performed:
- O Oath
- O Acknowledgment
- O Jurat
- O Other:

Identification:
- O I.D. Card
- O Drivers License
- O Passport
- O Other:
- O Credible Witness
- O Known Personally

I.D. Number:

Issued By:

Issued Date:

Expiration Date:

Document Type:

Date/Time Notarized: AM PM

Document Date:

Fee Charged:

Printed Name and Address of Witness:

Phone Number:

Email:

Witness' Signature:

Comments:

Record Number:
162

NOTARY RECORD

Printed Name and Address of Signer:

Phone Number:

Email:

Signer's Signature:

Thumb Print:

Service Performed:	Identification:		I.D. Number:	
O Oath	O I.D. Card	O Credible Witness		
O Acknowledgment	O Drivers License	O Known Personally	**Issued By:**	
O Jurat	O Passport		**Issued Date:**	**Expiration Date:**
O Other:	O Other:			

Document Type:	Date/Time Notarized:	AM PM	Document Date:	Fee Charged:

Printed Name and Address of Witness:

Phone Number:

Email:

Witness' Signature:

Comments:

Record Number:

163

NOTARY RECORD

Printed Name and Address of Signer:

Phone Number:

Email:

Signer's Signature:

Thumb Print:

Service Performed:	Identification:		I.D. Number:	
O Oath	O I.D. Card	O Credible Witness		
O Acknowledgment	O Drivers License	O Known Personally	**Issued By:**	
O Jurat	O Passport		**Issued Date:**	**Expiration Date:**
O Other:	O Other:			

Document Type:	Date/Time Notarized:	AM PM	Document Date:	Fee Charged:

Printed Name and Address of Witness:

Phone Number:

Email:

Witness' Signature:

Comments:

Record Number:

164

NOTARY RECORD

Printed Name and Address of Signer:

Phone Number:

Email:

Signer's Signature:

Thumb Print:

Service Performed:
- O Oath
- O Acknowledgment
- O Jurat
- O Other:

Identification:
- O I.D. Card
- O Drivers License
- O Passport
- O Other:
- O Credible Witness
- O Known Personally

I.D. Number:

Issued By:

Issued Date:

Expiration Date:

Document Type:

Date/Time Notarized: AM
                                  PM

Document Date:

Fee Charged:

Printed Name and Address of Witness:

Phone Number:

Email:

Witness' Signature:

Comments:

Record Number:
165

NOTARY RECORD

Printed Name and Address of Signer:

Phone Number:

Email:

Signer's Signature:

Thumb Print:

Service Performed:
- O Oath
- O Acknowledgment
- O Jurat
- O Other:

Identification:
- O I.D. Card
- O Drivers License
- O Passport
- O Other:
- O Credible Witness
- O Known Personally

I.D. Number:

Issued By:

Issued Date:

Expiration Date:

Document Type:

Date/Time Notarized: AM
                                  PM

Document Date:

Fee Charged:

Printed Name and Address of Witness:

Phone Number:

Email:

Witness' Signature:

Comments:

Record Number:
166

NOTARY RECORD

Printed Name and Address of Signer:

Phone Number:

Email:

Signer's Signature:

Thumb Print:

Service Performed:
- O Oath
- O Acknowledgment
- O Jurat
- O Other:

Identification:
- O I.D. Card
- O Drivers License
- O Passport
- O Other:
- O Credible Witness
- O Known Personally

I.D. Number:

Issued By:

Issued Date:

Expiration Date:

Document Type:

Date/Time Notarized: AM PM

Document Date:

Fee Charged:

Printed Name and Address of Witness:

Phone Number:

Email:

Witness' Signature:

Comments:

Record Number:
167

NOTARY RECORD

Printed Name and Address of Signer:

Phone Number:

Email:

Signer's Signature:

Thumb Print:

Service Performed:
- O Oath
- O Acknowledgment
- O Jurat
- O Other:

Identification:
- O I.D. Card
- O Drivers License
- O Passport
- O Other:
- O Credible Witness
- O Known Personally

I.D. Number:

Issued By:

Issued Date:

Expiration Date:

Document Type:

Date/Time Notarized: AM PM

Document Date:

Fee Charged:

Printed Name and Address of Witness:

Phone Number:

Email:

Witness' Signature:

Comments:

Record Number:
168

NOTARY RECORD

Printed Name and Address of Signer:

Phone Number:

Email:

Signer's Signature:

Thumb Print:

Service Performed:	Identification:		I.D. Number:	
O Oath	O I.D. Card	O Credible Witness		
O Acknowledgment	O Drivers License	O Known Personally	**Issued By:**	
O Jurat	O Passport		**Issued Date:**	**Expiration Date:**
O Other:	O Other:			

Document Type:	Date/Time Notarized:	AM PM	Document Date:	Fee Charged:

Printed Name and Address of Witness:

Phone Number:

Email:

Witness' Signature:

Comments:

Record Number:

169

NOTARY RECORD

Printed Name and Address of Signer:

Phone Number:

Email:

Signer's Signature:

Thumb Print:

Service Performed:	Identification:		I.D. Number:	
O Oath	O I.D. Card	O Credible Witness		
O Acknowledgment	O Drivers License	O Known Personally	**Issued By:**	
O Jurat	O Passport		**Issued Date:**	**Expiration Date:**
O Other:	O Other:			

Document Type:	Date/Time Notarized:	AM PM	Document Date:	Fee Charged:

Printed Name and Address of Witness:

Phone Number:

Email:

Witness' Signature:

Comments:

Record Number:

170

NOTARY RECORD

Printed Name and Address of Signer:

Phone Number:

Email:

Signer's Signature:

Thumb Print:

Service Performed:
- O Oath
- O Acknowledgment
- O Jurat
- O Other:

Identification:
- O I.D. Card
- O Drivers License
- O Passport
- O Other:
- O Credible Witness
- O Known Personally

I.D. Number:

Issued By:

Issued Date:

Expiration Date:

Document Type:

Date/Time Notarized: AM PM

Document Date:

Fee Charged:

Printed Name and Address of Witness:

Phone Number:

Email:

Witness' Signature:

Comments:

Record Number:
171

NOTARY RECORD

Printed Name and Address of Signer:

Phone Number:

Email:

Signer's Signature:

Thumb Print:

Service Performed:
- O Oath
- O Acknowledgment
- O Jurat
- O Other:

Identification:
- O I.D. Card
- O Drivers License
- O Passport
- O Other:
- O Credible Witness
- O Known Personally

I.D. Number:

Issued By:

Issued Date:

Expiration Date:

Document Type:

Date/Time Notarized: AM PM

Document Date:

Fee Charged:

Printed Name and Address of Witness:

Phone Number:

Email:

Witness' Signature:

Comments:

Record Number:
172

NOTARY RECORD

Printed Name and Address of Signer:

Phone Number:

Email:

Signer's Signature:

Thumb Print:

Service Performed:

O Oath

O Acknowledgment

O Jurat

O Other:

Identification:

O I.D. Card   O Credible Witness

O Drivers License   O Known Personally

O Passport

O Other:

I.D. Number:

Issued By:

Issued Date:

Expiration Date:

Document Type:

Date/Time Notarized: AM   PM

Document Date:

Fee Charged:

Printed Name and Address of Witness:

Phone Number:

Email:

Witness' Signature:

Comments:

Record Number:

173

NOTARY RECORD

Printed Name and Address of Signer:

Phone Number:

Email:

Signer's Signature:

Thumb Print:

Service Performed:

O Oath

O Acknowledgment

O Jurat

O Other:

Identification:

O I.D. Card   O Credible Witness

O Drivers License   O Known Personally

O Passport

O Other:

I.D. Number:

Issued By:

Issued Date:

Expiration Date:

Document Type:

Date/Time Notarized: AM   PM

Document Date:

Fee Charged:

Printed Name and Address of Witness:

Phone Number:

Email:

Witness' Signature:

Comments:

Record Number:

174

NOTARY RECORD

Printed Name and Address of Signer:	Phone Number:	Thumb Print:
	Email:	
	Signer's Signature:	

Service Performed:	Identification:	I.D. Number:	
O Oath	O I.D. Card O Credible Witness		
O Acknowledgment	O Drivers License O Known Personally	Issued By:	
O Jurat	O Passport	Issued Date:	Expiration Date:
O Other:	O Other:		

Document Type:	Date/Time Notarized: AM PM	Document Date:	Fee Charged:

Printed Name and Address of Witness:	Phone Number:
	Email:
	Witness' Signature:

Comments:	Record Number: **175**

NOTARY RECORD

Printed Name and Address of Signer:	Phone Number:	Thumb Print:
	Email:	
	Signer's Signature:	

Service Performed:	Identification:	I.D. Number:	
O Oath	O I.D. Card O Credible Witness		
O Acknowledgment	O Drivers License O Known Personally	Issued By:	
O Jurat	O Passport	Issued Date:	Expiration Date:
O Other:	O Other:		

Document Type:	Date/Time Notarized: AM PM	Document Date:	Fee Charged:

Printed Name and Address of Witness:	Phone Number:
	Email:
	Witness' Signature:

Comments:	Record Number: **176**

NOTARY RECORD

Printed Name and Address of Signer:

Phone Number:

Email:

Signer's Signature:

Thumb Print:

Service Performed:
- O Oath
- O Acknowledgment
- O Jurat
- O Other:

Identification:
- O I.D. Card
- O Drivers License
- O Passport
- O Other:
- O Credible Witness
- O Known Personally

I.D. Number:

Issued By:

Issued Date:

Expiration Date:

Document Type:

Date/Time Notarized: AM
                                    PM

Document Date:

Fee Charged:

Printed Name and Address of Witness:

Phone Number:

Email:

Witness' Signature:

Comments:

Record Number:
177

NOTARY RECORD

Printed Name and Address of Signer:

Phone Number:

Email:

Signer's Signature:

Thumb Print:

Service Performed:
- O Oath
- O Acknowledgment
- O Jurat
- O Other:

Identification:
- O I.D. Card
- O Drivers License
- O Passport
- O Other:
- O Credible Witness
- O Known Personally

I.D. Number:

Issued By:

Issued Date:

Expiration Date:

Document Type:

Date/Time Notarized: AM
                                    PM

Document Date:

Fee Charged:

Printed Name and Address of Witness:

Phone Number:

Email:

Witness' Signature:

Comments:

Record Number:
178

NOTARY RECORD

Printed Name and Address of Signer:	Phone Number:		Thumb Print:
	Email:		
	Signer's Signature:		

Service Performed:	Identification:		I.D. Number:	
O Oath	O I.D. Card	O Credible Witness		
O Acknowledgment	O Drivers License	O Known Personally	Issued By:	
O Jurat	O Passport		Issued Date:	Expiration Date:
O Other:	O Other:			

Document Type:	Date/Time Notarized:	AM PM	Document Date:	Fee Charged:

Printed Name and Address of Witness:	Phone Number:
	Email:
	Witness' Signature:

Comments:	Record Number: **179**

NOTARY RECORD

Printed Name and Address of Signer:	Phone Number:		Thumb Print:
	Email:		
	Signer's Signature:		

Service Performed:	Identification:		I.D. Number:	
O Oath	O I.D. Card	O Credible Witness		
O Acknowledgment	O Drivers License	O Known Personally	Issued By:	
O Jurat	O Passport		Issued Date:	Expiration Date:
O Other:	O Other:			

Document Type:	Date/Time Notarized:	AM PM	Document Date:	Fee Charged:

Printed Name and Address of Witness:	Phone Number:
	Email:
	Witness' Signature:

Comments:	Record Number: **180**

NOTARY RECORD

Printed Name and Address of Signer:	Phone Number:	Thumb Print:
	Email:	
	Signer's Signature:	

Service Performed:	Identification:	I.D. Number:	
O Oath	O I.D. Card O Credible Witness		
O Acknowledgment	O Drivers License O Known Personally	Issued By:	
O Jurat	O Passport	Issued Date:	Expiration Date:
O Other:	O Other:		

Document Type:	Date/Time Notarized: AM PM	Document Date:	Fee Charged:

Printed Name and Address of Witness:	Phone Number:
	Email:
	Witness' Signature:

Comments:	Record Number: **181**

NOTARY RECORD

Printed Name and Address of Signer:	Phone Number:	Thumb Print:
	Email:	
	Signer's Signature:	

Service Performed:	Identification:	I.D. Number:	
O Oath	O I.D. Card O Credible Witness		
O Acknowledgment	O Drivers License O Known Personally	Issued By:	
O Jurat	O Passport	Issued Date:	Expiration Date:
O Other:	O Other:		

Document Type:	Date/Time Notarized: AM PM	Document Date:	Fee Charged:

Printed Name and Address of Witness:	Phone Number:
	Email:
	Witness' Signature:

Comments:	Record Number: **182**

NOTARY RECORD

Printed Name and Address of Signer:	Phone Number:	Thumb Print:
	Email:	
	Signer's Signature:	

Service Performed:	Identification:	I.D. Number:	
O Oath	O I.D. Card O Credible Witness		
O Acknowledgment	O Drivers License O Known Personally	Issued By:	
O Jurat	O Passport	Issued Date:	Expiration Date:
O Other:	O Other:		

Document Type:	Date/Time Notarized: AM PM	Document Date:	Fee Charged:

Printed Name and Address of Witness:	Phone Number:
	Email:
	Witness' Signature:

Comments:	Record Number: **183**

NOTARY RECORD

Printed Name and Address of Signer:	Phone Number:	Thumb Print:
	Email:	
	Signer's Signature:	

Service Performed:	Identification:	I.D. Number:	
O Oath	O I.D. Card O Credible Witness		
O Acknowledgment	O Drivers License O Known Personally	Issued By:	
O Jurat	O Passport	Issued Date:	Expiration Date:
O Other:	O Other:		

Document Type:	Date/Time Notarized: AM PM	Document Date:	Fee Charged:

Printed Name and Address of Witness:	Phone Number:
	Email:
	Witness' Signature:

Comments:	Record Number: **184**

NOTARY RECORD

Printed Name and Address of Signer:

Phone Number:

Email:

Signer's Signature:

Thumb Print:

Service Performed:
- O Oath
- O Acknowledgment
- O Jurat
- O Other:

Identification:
- O I.D. Card
- O Drivers License
- O Passport
- O Other:
- O Credible Witness
- O Known Personally

I.D. Number:

Issued By:

Issued Date:

Expiration Date:

Document Type:

Date/Time Notarized: AM PM

Document Date:

Fee Charged:

Printed Name and Address of Witness:

Phone Number:

Email:

Witness' Signature:

Comments:

Record Number:
185

NOTARY RECORD

Printed Name and Address of Signer:

Phone Number:

Email:

Signer's Signature:

Thumb Print:

Service Performed:
- O Oath
- O Acknowledgment
- O Jurat
- O Other:

Identification:
- O I.D. Card
- O Drivers License
- O Passport
- O Other:
- O Credible Witness
- O Known Personally

I.D. Number:

Issued By:

Issued Date:

Expiration Date:

Document Type:

Date/Time Notarized: AM PM

Document Date:

Fee Charged:

Printed Name and Address of Witness:

Phone Number:

Email:

Witness' Signature:

Comments:

Record Number:
186

NOTARY RECORD

Printed Name and Address of Signer:	Phone Number:	Thumb Print:
	Email:	
	Signer's Signature:	

Service Performed:	Identification:	I.D. Number:	
O Oath	O I.D. Card O Credible Witness		
O Acknowledgment	O Drivers License O Known Personally	Issued By:	
O Jurat	O Passport	Issued Date:	Expiration Date:
O Other:	O Other:		

Document Type:	Date/Time Notarized: AM PM	Document Date:	Fee Charged:

Printed Name and Address of Witness:	Phone Number:
	Email:
	Witness' Signature:

Comments:	Record Number: **187**

NOTARY RECORD

Printed Name and Address of Signer:	Phone Number:	Thumb Print:
	Email:	
	Signer's Signature:	

Service Performed:	Identification:	I.D. Number:	
O Oath	O I.D. Card O Credible Witness		
O Acknowledgment	O Drivers License O Known Personally	Issued By:	
O Jurat	O Passport	Issued Date:	Expiration Date:
O Other:	O Other:		

Document Type:	Date/Time Notarized: AM PM	Document Date:	Fee Charged:

Printed Name and Address of Witness:	Phone Number:
	Email:
	Witness' Signature:

Comments:	Record Number: **188**

NOTARY RECORD

Printed Name and Address of Signer:

Phone Number:

Email:

Signer's Signature:

Thumb Print:

Service Performed:	Identification:		I.D. Number:	
O Oath	O I.D. Card	O Credible Witness		
O Acknowledgment	O Drivers License	O Known Personally	**Issued By:**	
O Jurat	O Passport		**Issued Date:**	**Expiration Date:**
O Other:	O Other:			

Document Type:	Date/Time Notarized:	AM PM	Document Date:	Fee Charged:

Printed Name and Address of Witness:

Phone Number:

Email:

Witness' Signature:

Comments:

Record Number:

189

NOTARY RECORD

Printed Name and Address of Signer:

Phone Number:

Email:

Signer's Signature:

Thumb Print:

Service Performed:	Identification:		I.D. Number:	
O Oath	O I.D. Card	O Credible Witness		
O Acknowledgment	O Drivers License	O Known Personally	**Issued By:**	
O Jurat	O Passport		**Issued Date:**	**Expiration Date:**
O Other:	O Other:			

Document Type:	Date/Time Notarized:	AM PM	Document Date:	Fee Charged:

Printed Name and Address of Witness:

Phone Number:

Email:

Witness' Signature:

Comments:

Record Number:

190

NOTARY RECORD

Printed Name and Address of Signer:

Phone Number:

Email:

Signer's Signature:

Thumb Print:

Service Performed:
- O Oath
- O Acknowledgment
- O Jurat
- O Other:

Identification:
- O I.D. Card
- O Drivers License
- O Passport
- O Other:
- O Credible Witness
- O Known Personally

I.D. Number:

Issued By:

Issued Date:

Expiration Date:

Document Type:

Date/Time Notarized: AM PM

Document Date:

Fee Charged:

Printed Name and Address of Witness:

Phone Number:

Email:

Witness' Signature:

Comments:

Record Number:
191

NOTARY RECORD

Printed Name and Address of Signer:

Phone Number:

Email:

Signer's Signature:

Thumb Print:

Service Performed:
- O Oath
- O Acknowledgment
- O Jurat
- O Other:

Identification:
- O I.D. Card
- O Drivers License
- O Passport
- O Other:
- O Credible Witness
- O Known Personally

I.D. Number:

Issued By:

Issued Date:

Expiration Date:

Document Type:

Date/Time Notarized: AM PM

Document Date:

Fee Charged:

Printed Name and Address of Witness:

Phone Number:

Email:

Witness' Signature:

Comments:

Record Number:
192

NOTARY RECORD

Printed Name and Address of Signer:

Phone Number:

Email:

Signer's Signature:

Thumb Print:

Service Performed:	Identification:		I.D. Number:	
O Oath	O I.D. Card	O Credible Witness		
O Acknowledgment	O Drivers License	O Known Personally	**Issued By:**	
O Jurat	O Passport		**Issued Date:**	**Expiration Date:**
O Other:	O Other:			

Document Type:	**Date/Time Notarized:** AM PM	**Document Date:**	**Fee Charged:**

Printed Name and Address of Witness:

Phone Number:

Email:

Witness' Signature:

Comments:

Record Number:

193

NOTARY RECORD

Printed Name and Address of Signer:

Phone Number:

Email:

Signer's Signature:

Thumb Print:

Service Performed:	Identification:		I.D. Number:	
O Oath	O I.D. Card	O Credible Witness		
O Acknowledgment	O Drivers License	O Known Personally	**Issued By:**	
O Jurat	O Passport		**Issued Date:**	**Expiration Date:**
O Other:	O Other:			

Document Type:	**Date/Time Notarized:** AM PM	**Document Date:**	**Fee Charged:**

Printed Name and Address of Witness:

Phone Number:

Email:

Witness' Signature:

Comments:

Record Number:

194

NOTARY RECORD

Printed Name and Address of Signer:	Phone Number:	Thumb Print:
	Email:	
	Signer's Signature:	

Service Performed:	Identification:	I.D. Number:	
O Oath	O I.D. Card O Credible Witness		
O Acknowledgment	O Drivers License O Known Personally	Issued By:	
O Jurat	O Passport	Issued Date:	Expiration Date:
O Other:	O Other:		

Document Type:	Date/Time Notarized: AM PM	Document Date:	Fee Charged:

Printed Name and Address of Witness:	Phone Number:
	Email:
	Witness' Signature:

Comments:	Record Number: **195**

NOTARY RECORD

Printed Name and Address of Signer:	Phone Number:	Thumb Print:
	Email:	
	Signer's Signature:	

Service Performed:	Identification:	I.D. Number:	
O Oath	O I.D. Card O Credible Witness		
O Acknowledgment	O Drivers License O Known Personally	Issued By:	
O Jurat	O Passport	Issued Date:	Expiration Date:
O Other:	O Other:		

Document Type:	Date/Time Notarized: AM PM	Document Date:	Fee Charged:

Printed Name and Address of Witness:	Phone Number:
	Email:
	Witness' Signature:

Comments:	Record Number: **196**

NOTARY RECORD

Printed Name and Address of Signer:	Phone Number:		Thumb Print:
	Email:		
	Signer's Signature:		

Service Performed:	Identification:		I.D. Number:	
O Oath	O I.D. Card	O Credible Witness		
O Acknowledgment	O Drivers License	O Known Personally	Issued By:	
O Jurat	O Passport		Issued Date:	Expiration Date:
O Other:	O Other:			

Document Type:	Date/Time Notarized:	AM PM	Document Date:	Fee Charged:

Printed Name and Address of Witness:	Phone Number:
	Email:
	Witness' Signature:

Comments:	Record Number:
	197

NOTARY RECORD

Printed Name and Address of Signer:	Phone Number:		Thumb Print:
	Email:		
	Signer's Signature:		

Service Performed:	Identification:		I.D. Number:	
O Oath	O I.D. Card	O Credible Witness		
O Acknowledgment	O Drivers License	O Known Personally	Issued By:	
O Jurat	O Passport		Issued Date:	Expiration Date:
O Other:	O Other:			

Document Type:	Date/Time Notarized:	AM PM	Document Date:	Fee Charged:

Printed Name and Address of Witness:	Phone Number:
	Email:
	Witness' Signature:

Comments:	Record Number:
	198

NOTARY RECORD

Printed Name and Address of Signer:	Phone Number:	Thumb Print:
	Email:	
	Signer's Signature:	

Service Performed:	Identification:	I.D. Number:	
O Oath	O I.D. Card O Credible Witness		
O Acknowledgment	O Drivers License O Known Personally	Issued By:	
O Jurat	O Passport	Issued Date:	Expiration Date:
O Other:	O Other:		

Document Type:	Date/Time Notarized: AM PM	Document Date:	Fee Charged:

Printed Name and Address of Witness:	Phone Number:
	Email:
	Witness' Signature:

Comments:	Record Number:
	199

NOTARY RECORD

Printed Name and Address of Signer:	Phone Number:	Thumb Print:
	Email:	
	Signer's Signature:	

Service Performed:	Identification:	I.D. Number:	
O Oath	O I.D. Card O Credible Witness		
O Acknowledgment	O Drivers License O Known Personally	Issued By:	
O Jurat	O Passport	Issued Date:	Expiration Date:
O Other:	O Other:		

Document Type:	Date/Time Notarized: AM PM	Document Date:	Fee Charged:

Printed Name and Address of Witness:	Phone Number:
	Email:
	Witness' Signature:

Comments:	Record Number:
	200

NOTARY RECORD

Printed Name and Address of Signer:

Phone Number:

Email:

Signer's Signature:

Thumb Print:

Service Performed:
- O Oath
- O Acknowledgment
- O Jurat
- O Other:

Identification:
- O I.D. Card
- O Drivers License
- O Passport
- O Other:
- O Credible Witness
- O Known Personally

I.D. Number:

Issued By:

Issued Date:

Expiration Date:

Document Type:

Date/Time Notarized: AM PM

Document Date:

Fee Charged:

Printed Name and Address of Witness:

Phone Number:

Email:

Witness' Signature:

Comments:

Record Number:
201

NOTARY RECORD

Printed Name and Address of Signer:

Phone Number:

Email:

Signer's Signature:

Thumb Print:

Service Performed:
- O Oath
- O Acknowledgment
- O Jurat
- O Other:

Identification:
- O I.D. Card
- O Drivers License
- O Passport
- O Other:
- O Credible Witness
- O Known Personally

I.D. Number:

Issued By:

Issued Date:

Expiration Date:

Document Type:

Date/Time Notarized: AM PM

Document Date:

Fee Charged:

Printed Name and Address of Witness:

Phone Number:

Email:

Witness' Signature:

Comments:

Record Number:
202

NOTARY RECORD

Printed Name and Address of Signer:	Phone Number:	Thumb Print:
	Email:	
	Signer's Signature:	

Service Performed:	Identification:	I.D. Number:	
O Oath	O I.D. Card O Credible Witness	Issued By:	
O Acknowledgment	O Drivers License O Known Personally		
O Jurat	O Passport	Issued Date:	Expiration Date:
O Other:	O Other:		

Document Type:	Date/Time Notarized:	AM PM	Document Date:	Fee Charged:

Printed Name and Address of Witness:	Phone Number:
	Email:
	Witness' Signature:

Comments:	Record Number: **203**

NOTARY RECORD

Printed Name and Address of Signer:	Phone Number:	Thumb Print:
	Email:	
	Signer's Signature:	

Service Performed:	Identification:	I.D. Number:	
O Oath	O I.D. Card O Credible Witness	Issued By:	
O Acknowledgment	O Drivers License O Known Personally		
O Jurat	O Passport	Issued Date:	Expiration Date:
O Other:	O Other:		

Document Type:	Date/Time Notarized:	AM PM	Document Date:	Fee Charged:

Printed Name and Address of Witness:	Phone Number:
	Email:
	Witness' Signature:

Comments:	Record Number: **204**

NOTARY RECORD

Printed Name and Address of Signer:

Phone Number:

Email:

Signer's Signature:

Thumb Print:

Service Performed:	Identification:		I.D. Number:
O Oath	O I.D. Card	O Credible Witness	
O Acknowledgment	O Drivers License	O Known Personally	**Issued By:**
O Jurat	O Passport		
O Other:	O Other:		**Issued Date:** / **Expiration Date:**

Document Type:	Date/Time Notarized: AM PM	Document Date:	Fee Charged:

Printed Name and Address of Witness:

Phone Number:

Email:

Witness' Signature:

Comments:

Record Number:
205

NOTARY RECORD

Printed Name and Address of Signer:

Phone Number:

Email:

Signer's Signature:

Thumb Print:

Service Performed:	Identification:		I.D. Number:
O Oath	O I.D. Card	O Credible Witness	
O Acknowledgment	O Drivers License	O Known Personally	**Issued By:**
O Jurat	O Passport		
O Other:	O Other:		**Issued Date:** / **Expiration Date:**

Document Type:	Date/Time Notarized: AM PM	Document Date:	Fee Charged:

Printed Name and Address of Witness:

Phone Number:

Email:

Witness' Signature:

Comments:

Record Number:
206

NOTARY RECORD

Printed Name and Address of Signer:	Phone Number:	Thumb Print:
	Email:	
	Signer's Signature:	

Service Performed:	Identification:		I.D. Number:
O Oath	O I.D. Card	O Credible Witness	
O Acknowledgment	O Drivers License	O Known Personally	Issued By:
O Jurat	O Passport		Issued Date: / Expiration Date:
O Other:	O Other:		

Document Type:	Date/Time Notarized: AM PM	Document Date:	Fee Charged:

Printed Name and Address of Witness:	Phone Number:
	Email:
	Witness' Signature:

Comments:	Record Number: **207**

NOTARY RECORD

Printed Name and Address of Signer:	Phone Number:	Thumb Print:
	Email:	
	Signer's Signature:	

Service Performed:	Identification:		I.D. Number:
O Oath	O I.D. Card	O Credible Witness	
O Acknowledgment	O Drivers License	O Known Personally	Issued By:
O Jurat	O Passport		Issued Date: / Expiration Date:
O Other:	O Other:		

Document Type:	Date/Time Notarized: AM PM	Document Date:	Fee Charged:

Printed Name and Address of Witness:	Phone Number:
	Email:
	Witness' Signature:

Comments:	Record Number: **208**

NOTARY RECORD

Printed Name and Address of Signer:

Phone Number:

Email:

Signer's Signature:

Thumb Print:

Service Performed:
- O Oath
- O Acknowledgment
- O Jurat
- O Other:

Identification:
- O I.D. Card
- O Drivers License
- O Passport
- O Other:
- O Credible Witness
- O Known Personally

I.D. Number:

Issued By:

Issued Date:

Expiration Date:

Document Type:

Date/Time Notarized: AM PM

Document Date:

Fee Charged:

Printed Name and Address of Witness:

Phone Number:

Email:

Witness' Signature:

Comments:

Record Number:
209

NOTARY RECORD

Printed Name and Address of Signer:

Phone Number:

Email:

Signer's Signature:

Thumb Print:

Service Performed:
- O Oath
- O Acknowledgment
- O Jurat
- O Other:

Identification:
- O I.D. Card
- O Drivers License
- O Passport
- O Other:
- O Credible Witness
- O Known Personally

I.D. Number:

Issued By:

Issued Date:

Expiration Date:

Document Type:

Date/Time Notarized: AM PM

Document Date:

Fee Charged:

Printed Name and Address of Witness:

Phone Number:

Email:

Witness' Signature:

Comments:

Record Number:
210

NOTARY RECORD

Printed Name and Address of Signer:	Phone Number:	Thumb Print:
	Email:	
	Signer's Signature:	

Service Performed:	Identification:	I.D. Number:	
O Oath	O I.D. Card O Credible Witness		
O Acknowledgment	O Drivers License O Known Personally	Issued By:	
O Jurat	O Passport		
O Other:	O Other:	Issued Date:	Expiration Date:

Document Type:	Date/Time Notarized: AM PM	Document Date:	Fee Charged:

Printed Name and Address of Witness:	Phone Number:
	Email:
	Witness' Signature:

Comments:	Record Number: **211**

NOTARY RECORD

Printed Name and Address of Signer:	Phone Number:	Thumb Print:
	Email:	
	Signer's Signature:	

Service Performed:	Identification:	I.D. Number:	
O Oath	O I.D. Card O Credible Witness		
O Acknowledgment	O Drivers License O Known Personally	Issued By:	
O Jurat	O Passport		
O Other:	O Other:	Issued Date:	Expiration Date:

Document Type:	Date/Time Notarized: AM PM	Document Date:	Fee Charged:

Printed Name and Address of Witness:	Phone Number:
	Email:
	Witness' Signature:

Comments:	Record Number: **212**

NOTARY RECORD

Printed Name and Address of Signer:

Phone Number:

Email:

Signer's Signature:

Thumb Print:

Service Performed:
- O Oath
- O Acknowledgment
- O Jurat
- O Other:

Identification:
- O I.D. Card
- O Drivers License
- O Passport
- O Other:
- O Credible Witness
- O Known Personally

I.D. Number:

Issued By:

Issued Date:

Expiration Date:

Document Type:

Date/Time Notarized: AM   PM

Document Date:

Fee Charged:

Printed Name and Address of Witness:

Phone Number:

Email:

Witness' Signature:

Comments:

Record Number:
213

NOTARY RECORD

Printed Name and Address of Signer:

Phone Number:

Email:

Signer's Signature:

Thumb Print:

Service Performed:
- O Oath
- O Acknowledgment
- O Jurat
- O Other:

Identification:
- O I.D. Card
- O Drivers License
- O Passport
- O Other:
- O Credible Witness
- O Known Personally

I.D. Number:

Issued By:

Issued Date:

Expiration Date:

Document Type:

Date/Time Notarized: AM   PM

Document Date:

Fee Charged:

Printed Name and Address of Witness:

Phone Number:

Email:

Witness' Signature:

Comments:

Record Number:
214

NOTARY RECORD

Printed Name and Address of Signer:	Phone Number:	Thumb Print:
	Email:	
	Signer's Signature:	

Service Performed:	Identification:	I.D. Number:	
O Oath	O I.D. Card O Credible Witness		
O Acknowledgment	O Drivers License O Known Personally	Issued By:	
O Jurat	O Passport	Issued Date:	Expiration Date:
O Other:	O Other:		

Document Type:	Date/Time Notarized: AM PM	Document Date:	Fee Charged:

Printed Name and Address of Witness:	Phone Number:
	Email:
	Witness' Signature:

Comments:	Record Number: 215

NOTARY RECORD

Printed Name and Address of Signer:	Phone Number:	Thumb Print:
	Email:	
	Signer's Signature:	

Service Performed:	Identification:	I.D. Number:	
O Oath	O I.D. Card O Credible Witness		
O Acknowledgment	O Drivers License O Known Personally	Issued By:	
O Jurat	O Passport	Issued Date:	Expiration Date:
O Other:	O Other:		

Document Type:	Date/Time Notarized: AM PM	Document Date:	Fee Charged:

Printed Name and Address of Witness:	Phone Number:
	Email:
	Witness' Signature:

Comments:	Record Number: 216

NOTARY RECORD

Printed Name and Address of Signer:	Phone Number:	Thumb Print:
	Email:	
	Signer's Signature:	

Service Performed:	Identification:	I.D. Number:	
O Oath	O I.D. Card O Credible Witness		
O Acknowledgment	O Drivers License O Known Personally	Issued By:	
O Jurat	O Passport	Issued Date:	Expiration Date:
O Other:	O Other:		

Document Type:	Date/Time Notarized: AM PM	Document Date:	Fee Charged:

Printed Name and Address of Witness:	Phone Number:
	Email:
	Witness' Signature:

Comments:	Record Number: **217**

NOTARY RECORD

Printed Name and Address of Signer:	Phone Number:	Thumb Print:
	Email:	
	Signer's Signature:	

Service Performed:	Identification:	I.D. Number:	
O Oath	O I.D. Card O Credible Witness		
O Acknowledgment	O Drivers License O Known Personally	Issued By:	
O Jurat	O Passport	Issued Date:	Expiration Date:
O Other:	O Other:		

Document Type:	Date/Time Notarized: AM PM	Document Date:	Fee Charged:

Printed Name and Address of Witness:	Phone Number:
	Email:
	Witness' Signature:

Comments:	Record Number: **218**

NOTARY RECORD

Printed Name and Address of Signer:	**Phone Number:**	**Thumb Print:**
	Email:	
	Signer's Signature:	

Service Performed:	**Identification:**	**I.D. Number:**	
O Oath	O I.D. Card O Credible Witness		
O Acknowledgment	O Drivers License O Known Personally	**Issued By:**	
O Jurat	O Passport	**Issued Date:**	**Expiration Date:**
O Other:	O Other:		

Document Type:	**Date/Time Notarized:** AM PM	**Document Date:**	**Fee Charged:**

Printed Name and Address of Witness:	**Phone Number:**
	Email:
	Witness' Signature:

Comments:	**Record Number:** **219**

NOTARY RECORD

Printed Name and Address of Signer:	**Phone Number:**	**Thumb Print:**
	Email:	
	Signer's Signature:	

Service Performed:	**Identification:**	**I.D. Number:**	
O Oath	O I.D. Card O Credible Witness		
O Acknowledgment	O Drivers License O Known Personally	**Issued By:**	
O Jurat	O Passport	**Issued Date:**	**Expiration Date:**
O Other:	O Other:		

Document Type:	**Date/Time Notarized:** AM PM	**Document Date:**	**Fee Charged:**

Printed Name and Address of Witness:	**Phone Number:**
	Email:
	Witness' Signature:

Comments:	**Record Number:** **220**

Made in the USA
Columbia, SC
28 January 2021